ROMY GR...

BOLOGNA
a city to discover

Museum texts by
ORIANO TASSINARI CLÒ

Published by
ITALCARDS
bologna Italy

Sole distributor for Bologna and its province
Via S. Pio V, 19/A - ☎ 550487 - 40131 BOLOGNA

*This book
is dedicated to the memory of
Commendatore Gaetano Orlandi
founder of
Fotometalgrafica Emiliana*

Graphics and layout:
Federico Frassinetti

Photography by:
Ascanio Ascani / Forlì

Other photos by:
CNB & C.

The photos on page 60 are from Father Antonio Pinci of the Basilica of San Martino.

ITALCARDS Publisher
© Copyright by La Fotometalgrafica Emiliana Spa
All rights reserved
Any reproduction, even partial, is prohibited.

On the title page: Michelangelo's St. Petronius, detail of the Sarcophagus in the Basilica Sanctuary of St. Dominic.

Pages 4 and 5. The «heart» of the historic center between St. Peter's and St. Petronius. Beyond the Two Towers, the ray-like streets to the East.

Introduction

For the convenience of the tourist, we have divided the city into four parts, making use, for the sake of necessity, of natural subdivisions. These are formed by the oldest Bolognese artery, the via Emilia (which in the historic centre becomes via San Felice, via Ugo Bassi, via Rizzoli and strada Maggiore) and the relatively modern via Indipendenza whose natural continuation is formed by piazza Nettuno, piazza Maggiore and via d'Azeglio.

From the crossing-point of these roads, and in the shadow of one of the most famous symbols of the city, Neptune's fountain which the Bolognese familiarly call «the giant», we will therefore begin the first of the four itineraries of the city. We will however consider this cross-roads as a reference point for the other three itineraries too, thus allowing the tourist to orientate himself more easily.

To see it in a thorough and practical way, the city should be visited on foot. The distances are not excessive and, considering the various halts that the tourist can make between visits, he should not be too tired at the end of each day's tour.

One suggestion: the complete visit can be undertaken in four or five days in such a way as to get to know the most interesting aspects sufficiently, from the artistic and historic point of view, of this important Emilian centre. A day each can be dedicated to the first two itineraries. The third and the fourth can be subdivided in two days or in a morning and an afternoon of the same day, one prefers. For the countryside around Bologna, interesting and pleasant particularly in good weather, even only one day can suffice... or, considering its characteristics, one day each. Bologna is a welcoming city and full of good reasons for convincing even the most sceptical tourist to prolong his stay. Before moving on to the first itinerary, here are some interesting facts about the city. Bologna is one of the most «porticoed» cities in existence: this typical architecture in fact extends for approximately 35 kilometres. Even modern buildings have in fact tended to respect this ancient city characteristic, so that the innumerable porticoes of the past are joined by those of the present.

Another important feature is that of the towers: as well as the two most famous ones, which, together with Neptune, symbolize the city, there are about twenty more; originally, however, it seems that there were more than 150 and during restructuring operations in some old palazzi, the foundations of some of these lost constructions have come to light.

Finally the walls. As will be seen by following the various itineraries, it is possible to see how there were various circles, today absorbed into the body of the city. Those still visible are the most recent and they were built around the middle of the XIII century. The others, receding more and more towards the heart of the city, are evidence of its expansion through the centuries. They are attributed respectively to the XII century (circle of the «gate-towers») and to the VIII century (circle of the selenites). The most recent were partly demolished at the beginning of the present century: there are however large sections still standing and above all the «gates», whic for the Bolognese even today, are the most useful reference point to subdivide the city (via such-and-such? It's outside the... X gate, and near the... Y gate).

History

The origins of Bologna contain several fascinating aspects: that touch of mystery, those traces of ancient history which bear witness to a dignified past, so much artistic and sumptuous wealth, mix together to form a cocktail which it is difficult to remain indifferent to.

The mystery: the origins of the city are to be found around the IX century B.C. From that period come the remains of the Villanovian civilization which takes its name from Villanova di Castenaso, a settlement not far from the city, the present state road San Vitale, which leads to Ravenna. This iron-age civilization was followed by the Etruscan civilization, to which Bologna owes its ancient name, Felzna, then Felsinea. The fascination of the Etruscans and the aura which surrounds their obscure past, thus throw a suggestive light over the early life of the city which was long considered the capital of the Etruscan Po valley plain.

Around the VI century and up to about the mid IV century B.C., Felsina thus enjoyed a period of extreme prosperity, which suddenly came to a stop when the Celtic tribes invaded Etruria, after having crossed the Po. These tribes, living by agriculture and war, imposed a new regime on the life of the community, the Boian Gauls also settled in Felsina. These probably originated from Gaul, but some say they originate from Bohemia.

Is it from here that the new name of the city derives? Who knows? Some say it could be so, since the denomination of the Boian tribe is at the roots of the name Bononia, then Bologna. But it is perhaps more probable that the name of the city was born, two centuries later, with the coming of the Romans. They in fact then had a prospering colony at Ariminum, the present day Rimini, and enlarging their dominion over a good part of the Po valley plain, they laid hands on the ancient Felsina. Around the year 190 B.C., Publius Cornelius Scipio Nasica, cousin of Scipio the African, drove out the Boian Gauls and, shortly after, the Roman Senate charged three magistrates with the task of dividing up a territory of about 400 square kilometres between the three thousand colonists who came there to found a new latin city. Each new settlement was given the inauguration name of «bona», from bonus, by the Romans. Therefore Bononia could derive from this term. Soon after the city was founded, a great new road was created to connect the city to Rome. This was the via Emilia, which even today with a few name changes only in the historical centre, cuts the city in two.

Bononia then underwent a relatively tranquil period of expansion until 53 A.D., wen it was almost completely razed to the ground by a fire. Oddly enough, the person who intervened for its reconstruction was no other than Nero, who later resorted to fire with a much different spirit. Thanks to him, the Emperor Claudio, whose adopted son he was, had the city reconstructed. And in fact, in less than twenty years, Bononia rose again. With the ebb of the Roman influence, in 476 the city became part of the Gothic Kingdom of Odoacre, but less than a century later, as a result of the Greek-Gothic war, it came under Byzantine dominion, as did most of the peninsula.

And so it remained, with various

The protruding towers and bell-towers are characteristic of Bologna's skyline.

events, until the arrival of the Lombards and their definitive settling in Emilia in 727. This domination did not last long however: 774 brought the arrival of the Franks of Charlemagne, who soon after «yelded» the city to Pontifical rule.

In spite of being subdued by the Papacy, the city managed to maintain its own political character for many years. And so we arrive at 1116, when, a year after the death of Matilde di Canossa, whose influence was also felt on Bolognese events, the inhabitants rebelled and obtained permission by Enrico V to establish the town council. The city gained new impetus (the University was founded in this period) and widened its influence over the surrounding countryside. In the meantime however, Federico Barbarossa, was subduing the various cities of Lombardy and Veneto with his magistrates and consuls. In contrast to this, the Lombardy League was set up, to which Bologna also adhered. The construction of a new circle of walls (of which even today various parts are still preserved, the «gate towers») goes back to this period. This enlarged the fortifications, partly demolished by Barbarossa himself, which previously existed, the so-called «circle of selenite» (of natural chalk) of the VIII century. In 1176, Barbarossa was defeated at Legnano.

After the peace treaty of Costance, the Italian cities fought to obtain the indipendence conceded to them in that treaty, and Bologna was one of these. In the battle of Fossalta in 1249, the Bolognese army defeated that of Federico II, capturing his natural son, Enzo, King of Sardinia. He was brought to Bologna in chains and left to die in prison, though with every possible comfort, in the palazzo which even today is named after him. His tomb is in the church of San Domenico. Then follows a period of various events on the city's behalf, of bloody battles for predominance of local power. This however did not obstruct the building of churches and «palazzi». The churches of San Francesco, Santa Maria dei Servi, San Giacomo, San Domenico etc., were constructed in this period. And so we arrive at the period of dominion by the great families, with the splendour and prestige of various houses, the most important of which was the house of Bentivoglio. This family held the reins of Bologna until 1506, when the city, shaken by all kinds of tragedy, again passed under the papal rule of Giulio II. The Bentivoglios tried again several times to retake the city, but in vain. Pontifical supremacy over the city did in fact persist until the effects of the French revolution touched it from nearby. In 1796 Bologna was invaded by the Republican troops alternated with the Austrians on three occasions until 1816, when the city came again under the dominion of the Church. This lasted for a short period. In 1831 the Austrians again occupied the city and after being driven from it and reoccupying it on numerous occasions (a famous example is the popular revolt of 1848), they stayed until the proclamation of the Roman republic followed by the end of the temporal power of the Church over the city which, in 1860, by a plebiscite, was annexed to the Kingdom of Savoy. The life of the city, particularly from the political point of view, was extremely lively and thus it remained until just before the First World War. Towards the end of the last century various newspapers were founded, one of which, the Resto del Carlino, still preserving its original name, is amongst the oldest in Italy (1885). The 1915-18 War left its mark on the city, with a series of social problems which continued for a long time and were used to politically influence the Bolognese. The second World War increased Bologna's problems: it was shaken by 43 bombardments. Then, the German occupation, the beginning of the Resistance, the Liberation, the slow revival, its new appearance, that of today. This appearance is that of a city which is modern, refined, enterprising, full of vital turmoil, of cultural and economic initiatives. Among these should be remembered the numerous exhibitions of the Local Organization for the Fairs of Bologna (in order, from the beginning of the year, the Exhibition for sports installations and equipment, the SAIT Fashion Knitwear Exhibition, Fashion Footwear Exhibition, the Promac, exhibition of equipment and systems for machine and plant design; the Children's Book Fair, the Exhibition of perfumes and cosmetics, the SARP, tire and equipment exhibition; the Foodstuffs Exhibition and the International Fair, the Micam, International footwear exhibition, the second autumnal edition of SAIT Fashion Knitwear, the SAIE, building industry exhibition; the Exhibition of the agricultural machine industries, the Motor Show and the Boat Show, exhibitions respectively of international motoring and navigation), the scientific and cultural initiatives of the University, the medical and economic congresses, etc. A city to be discovered and with which to make friends quickly. The cordiality of the people «bridges» the gap for anyone coming from «outside the city gates».

Via d'Azeglio, looking towards the Clock Tower.

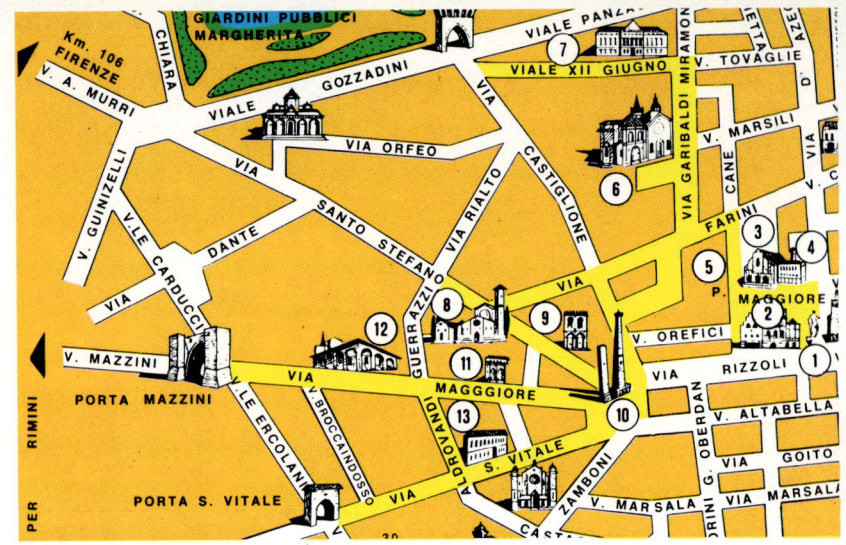

1st Itinerary

Summary:

1 Fountain of Neptune
2 Palazzo Re Enzo and Palazzo del Podestà
3 Basilica of St. Petronius
4 Palazzo dei Notai
5 Civic Archaeological Museum, Museum of the First and Second Risorgimento, and Archiginnasio
6 Basilica of St. Dominic
7 Palace of Justice
8 Complex of the Churches of St. Stephen
9 Merchants' Palace
10 Due Torri
11 Casa Isolani
12 Church of St. Mary of the Servants
13 Palazzo Fantuzzi

We will begin with **Neptune's fountain**, a famous Renaissance work of art. It was realized by the Flemish Giambologna in 1556, based on the project of Laureti the architect. Turning our backs on Neptune, on our right we see the Palazzo d'Accursio, which we will ignore for the moment, and on our left the **Palazzo Re Enzo**.

The construction of this building goes back to the first half of the 13th century 1200. It is named after the son of Federico II, Enzo, King of Sardinia, who was kept prisoner there for 23 years until his death, after having been defeated at the battle of Fossalta in 1249. The building was originally meant to house the The Deeds Chamber which holds the Archives of the town Notary; while in the adjoining **Palazzo del Podestà** the council meetings were held. On the ground floor, **the Carroccio** was kept (an ox-cart which accompanied the army and bore in altar, a bell and the standard of an Italian Commune of the Middle Ages). This was the symbol of the Commune and during battles it was defended by a group of young men of the most important families of the city. The chapel of Santa Maria dei Carcerati (St. Mary of the prisoners) can be seen in the courtyard of this building and was constructed after the building itself was finished. It served to give extreme unc-

1. The busy area of the Palazzo del Podestà and Palazzo Re Enzo. 2. The famous monumental Fountain by Giambologna. 3. Piazza Maggiore, the admirable artistic and civic heart of the city.

1

2

tion to those who, on leaving the prison, were taken away to be executed.

Leaving Palazzo Re Enzo and turning left immediately we come out into the beautiful **piazza Maggiore**, heart of the city, which even today is the meeting-place for all events — both gay and sad — of the community. Look around and admire the harmonious and impressive whole of the buildings which face onto the square, forming a unique framework for the richness of detail. Facing us and slightly towards the right, is the **palazzetto dei Notai** (palaz-

zo of the Notaries) which housed one of the many «corporations» existing in the city in the XVI century, its construction goes back to 1381 and it now houses private offices.

Directly in front of us is the marvellous **basilica of San Petronio**, the façade of which is incomplete. The marble base, recently restored, forms its only ornament. The construction of this religious building began in 1390 based on the project by the Bolognese mastro Antonio di Vincenzo, who was also responsible for the marble base. Its dimensions are among the most notable in the world: 132.60 metres in length, 60 metres wide, 48 metres high. It should however have been even bigger, in the form of a latin cross. To get some idea of the initial project, a wooden model made by Arduino Arriguzzi in 1514 can be seen in the small muse-

1. Palazzo dei Notai, 13th-15th C. Basilica of St. Petronius. 2. The incomplete façade of St. Petronius defines the southern side of Piazza Maggiore. 3. Porta Magna, masterpiece by Jacopo della Quercia. 4. Left side of the basilica in Via dell'Archiginnasio. 5. Panel by Jacopo della Quercia, «Original Sin». 6. St. Dominic's marble base.

15

um in the Basilica. The style is Italian Gothic. In the fanlight over the entrance, the Madonna with Child and the San Petronio are by Jacopo della Quercia, who was also responsible for the beautiful panels of the main door.

Inside the church, twelve slender pillars rise up to the roof and the arches are ogival. There are twenty-two chapels, some of which are authentic works of art. The first on the left is that of Sant'Abbondio, with frescoes by Giovanni da Modena. The second is that of San Petronio, formerly Aldrovandi and even before that, Griffoni. The bas-reliefs of the lateral walls are by the brothers Ottavio and Nicola Toselli. The marble statue of Cardinal Aldrovandi is by Angelo Piò and Camillo Rusconi. The pictures are by Vittorio Bigari and Stefano Orlandi. The third chapel is dedicated to Sant'Ivo. The canvases are by Gaetano Gandolfi, Alessandro Tiarini and Francesco Brizzi. The frescoes are by Pietro Lianori and Jacopo di Paolo.

The fourth chapel, dedicated to the Magi, has a marble transenna attributed to Antonio di Vincenzo. The precious wooden panel painting has a predella by Jacopo di Paolo which recounts the journey of the magi to Bethlehem. The same theme is depicted on the walls by Giovanni da Modena. The fifth chapel is that of San Sebastiano, with canvases by Jacopo Ripandà, by Costa, and stained glass windows by Giacomo Cabrini. The sixth chapel, dedicated to San Vincenzo, has a large tempera by Vittorio Bigari. Here is part of a famous polyptych by Francesco del Cossa, since split up, and now in various museums throughout Europe and America. The bronze statue of Cardinal Lercaro, beloved archbishop of the city until the 60's, is by Giacomo Manzù. The seventh chapel is dedicated to San Giacomo, with an oil painting on wood by Lorenzo Costa. Elisa Bonaparte, Napoleon's sister, together with her husband, Felice Baciocchi, is buried here in the tomb on the right.

Between the seventh and eigth chapel, is the tomb of the Bolognese bishop Nacci, and the memorial stone recording the construction of the famous and perfect meridian line which can be noted on the door of the church. This was designed and realized by Gian Domenico Cassini.

Basilica of St. Petronius: 1. Harmony and light inside St. Petronius. 2. Giovanni da Modena: The tree of the Cross in the Old and New Testaments. 3. Peter and Alberico: stone cross (1159). 4. Bolognini Chapel, decorated 1400-1420. 5. Chapel of St. Sebastian: stained glass windows designed by Costa (15th C.).

On the altar of the eigth chapel, dedicated to San Rocco, is a canvas by Parmigianino, depicting the Saint. The ninth chapel is that of San Michele, with a canvas by the Flemish Calvaert and terracotta busts by Vincenzo Onofri. In the tenth chapel, dedicated to Santa Barbara, the canvas is by Alessandro Tiarini; the statue, of Santa Rosalia, is by Gabriele Brunelli whilst the frescoes are by Gioacchino Pizzoli. The eleventh chapel, dedicated to San Bernardino, houses a wooden statue of the Saint, realised in the

1400's, of uncertain author, and paintings by Amico Aspertini.

Between this and the next chapel, is the door to the museum of the Basilica. This houses the architectural drawings made to complete the unfinished façade of the church and which carries the signatures of Andrea Palladio, Domenico da Varignana, Vignola, Terribilia, etc. There is also a relief of Milan Cathedral done by Antonio di Vincenzo and the wooden model of how the Basilica of San Petronio should have been, according to Arriguzzi.

We finally come to the main chapel. The wooden crucifix of the XV century, is surmounted by a «gallery» in marble and wood of the XVII century, designed by Vignola. The two organs, of different periods, are, respectively, the righ-thand one with Gothic inlays, by Lorenzo da Prato (1476), and the left-hand one by Baldassarre Malamini (1596). The choir consists of 85 upper stalls and 47 lower stalls and was constructed in 1477 by Agostino de' Marchi. The apse, with the Virgin and San Petronio, is by Marcantonio Franceschini.

But returning to the side chapels, the twelfth is that «of the Relics». The belltower of the church rises above this chapel. The Assumption is by the Veronese Domenico Rizzi, known as the Brusasorci. The thirteenth chapel, dedicated to San Pietro Martire, has a canvas by Passarotti and paintings by Francesco Brizzi. The fourteenth, dedicated to Sant'Antonio da Padova, has a statue and paintings by Girolamo da Treviso, while higher up the decorations are by Fulgenzio Mondini and Giacomo Alboresi. The stained glass windows were designed by Pellegrino Tibaldi. Next comes the fifteenth chapel, dedicated to the Holy Sacrament. The niche above the altar was designed by Vignola. The statues are by Nicolò da Milano and Zaccaria da Volterra; the tabernacle, made of hard stone, is by Vincenzo Franceschini; the inlaid stalls by the monk Raffaele da Brescia, Olivetano. The canvases are by Pasinelli and Mastelletta. The sixteenth chapel is that of the Immaculate Virgin, with a stucco-work statue by Corsini and modern decoration by Achille Casanova. The seventeenth is to San Girolamo. The oil painting on the al-

Basilica of St. Petronius: 1. St. Rocco, by Parmigianino. 2. Sacramental Chapel: St. Petronius, tarsia by Raffaele da Brescia. 3. The main apse.

tar is probably by Lorenzo Costa; the terracotta statue of the Madonna is by Giulio Romano. The eighteenth chapel, to San Lorenzo, has a canvas on the altar by Amico Aspertini and, on the right, by Jacopo Alessandro Calvi. The crucifix is from the XV century. The nineteenth chapel, of the Cross, has a beautiful stained glass window by Michele di Matteo. The paintings are by Francesco Lola and Francesco da Rimini and the frescoes by Lippo Dalmasio and Pietro Lianori.

The twentieth chapel, dedicated to Sant'Ambrogio, has a Venetian style polyptych of uncertain author and a stained glass window of the 1500's. The twenty-first chapel is that of Santa Brigida, with an oil-panting on wood by Tommaso Garelli and frescoes by Luca da Perugia and Francesco Lola. Finally we come to the twenty-second and last chapel, dedicated to the Madonna of Peace, with an XVIII century altar-piece into which is set an XIV century Madonna with Child by Giovanni Ferrabech. The frontal was painted by Giacomo Francia.

On completing the visit to San Petronio, pause for a moment on the steps which dominate the square to admire the beautiful and striking view which meets the eye on looking around. Then cross the big square pavement at the centre of the square itself and which the Bolognese familiarly call «crescentone» from the name of a rustic food, the crescente, typical in Emilia, to get a closer look at the facing **Palazzo del Podestà**, of the XIII century with decorations and a portico with the characteristic «ashlar» (bugnato) of 1470. Inside the large upper hall, frescoes by De Carolis. Towering above it is the XIII century **Arengo Tower** with a bell weighing 47 quintals, hoisted into placed by Fioravanti.

Turning our backs on the Palazzo del Podestà and facing San Petronio again, on our left we see the **Pavaglione** portico, ancient and modern walking place for the Bolognese. Its dialect name, pavajan, comes from a French term «pavillon», or rather pavillon, under which the market was held in the past. From the dialect name, the word has become Italianized. The portico, however, is that of the **Palazzo dei Ban-**

chi (of the Stalls), whose splendid façade was designed by Jacopo Barozzi, known as «il Vignola», in 1565. Before walking the length of the «Pavaglione» and admiring amongst other things, the many elegant shops, it is worth while making a short sedour to the left in via Clavature, to visit the **church of Santa Maria della Vita**. Built in the XVII century, it is surmounted by a beautiful copper dome which was built in the following century on the design of Bibiena. Inside the church is a famous terracotta group, known as the crying Marys, by Nicolò dell'Arca.

On leaving the church and turning back into the Pavaglione, we reach, after only a few yards, the **Civic Archaeological Museum** housed in the XV century «hospital of St. Mary of the Dead», whose portico was realized by Terribilia. The museum is worth a lengthy visit as it presents a vast and rich archaeological documentation from prehistory to the Roman era. There are also sections dedicated to Greece and Egypt. In the same building is a famous restoration workshop and a library containing about 4,000 volumes. After leaving the museum and retracting our steps for a few yards along the Pavaglione, on the right we come to the entrance of the **Museum of**

1. Palazzo del Podestà and the Arengo tower.
2. Bank Palace, by Vignola. 3. Church of Santa Maria della Vita.

the 1st and 2nd Risorgimento, founded at the end of the last century. Here we can see collections of arms, uniforms, flags, portraits, etc., and a specialist library containing approximately 50.000 volumes. Turning back along the Pavaglione, and shortly after the entrance to the Archaeological Museum, is the famous **Archiginnasio Museum**, also by Terribilia, realized in the mid XVI century to unite the various University faculties. The splendid courtyard, square and with a double open gallery, is decorated by the coats-of-arms of rectors, lecturers and students who taught or studied there. Inside and facing the entrance is the **chapel of Santa Maria dei Bulgari** (St. Mary of the Bulgarians) which was almost destroyed during a bombardment in 1944 and which was then restored. The church contains fragments of frescoes salvaged from the rubble in whic other works of art were lost. The

anatomical theatre, of the XVII century, was also damaged during the same bombardment. It was reconstructed and is still today a great cultural attraction due to the unusual solutions adopted during its construction. The upper floors contain the great communal library housing approximately half a million volumes. On leaving the Archiginnasio, we continue to the end of the Pavaglione. Then, turning left, we go along via Farini for a short while, until we reach piazza Cavour. Keeping to the right, we then come into via Garibaldi and, after a few yards, we have a splendid view on the left of the **Basilica of San Domenico**, which houses the tomb of the Saint. Begun immediately after his death, in 1221, on the church of San Nicolò delle Vigne, it underwent enlargements and re-arrangements practically right up to the beginning of this century, when a portico built in the 1700's was removed

1.2.3. Church of Santa Maria della Vita: Pietà and details, by Nicolò dell'Arca, terracotta (1463). 4. Hall of the Bolognese Necropolis. 5. Ugo Bassi in the Comacchio prison (5 August 1849), by C. Ademolio.

23

from the façade. It was originally divided in two parts, one reserved for the friars of the convent, the other for the Bolognese worshippers, then joined together around 1730. Inside the church, are beautiful chapels (among which is the one housing the remains

1. The Archiginnasio, by Terribilia (1562-63). 2. The dual-gallery courtyard. 3. Aula Magna of the Jurists, known as the Hall of the Stabat Mater. 4. Anatomical theatre (16th C.).

of the Saint and the one where King Enzo is buried) with works by great masters: Filippo Lippi, Guercino, Guido Reni (who is buried here), Ludovico Carracci, etc.

In the square is the tomb of Rolandino de' Passeggeri, famous jurisprudent of 1200. On the two columns are the statues of San Domenico and the Madonna of the Rosary, both in copper and respectively of 1627 and 1632. Continuing along via Garibaldi for a few yards more, we find ourselves in front of the present **Palazzo di Giustizia** (Law Courts), formerly Palazzo Baciocchi and before that again,

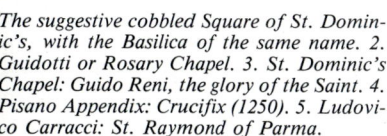

The suggestive cobbled Square of St. Dominic's, with the Basilica of the same name. 2. Guidotti or Rosary Chapel. 3. St. Dominic's Chapel: Guido Reni, the glory of the Saint. 4. Pisano Appendix: Crucifix (1250). 5. Ludovico Carracci: St. Raymond of Parma.

27

28

St. Dominic's Basilica: 1. The beautiful Arc, crafted between the 13th and 18th centuries. 2. Angel, by Nicolò dell'Arca. 3. Angel by Michelangelo. 4. The cloister (14th-15th C). 5. Mausoleum by Rolandino Passeggeri at St. Dominic's.

Ranuzzi-Ruini, constructed by Palladio in 1584. Elisa Bonaparte, Napoleon's sister wife of Prince Baciocchi, lived here at one time.

Returning along via Garibaldi, we come back to piazza Cavour and, turning right along via Farini, we reach **piazza Minghetti** containing the statue of the famous Bolognese statesman. On the right is the **palazzo of the Cassa di Risparmio** (Savings Bank), built in 1876 by Mengoni, who is also responsible for the Galleria in Milan. On the left is the **palazzo Policardi**, formerly Cac-

29

cianemici, of the XIII century, with the Passipoveri tower of the XII century. The nearby Vault goes back to the Middle Ages.

Continuing again along via Farini, on the right is a short street leading up to the **church of San Giovanni in Monte** (next to which is the prison today) of the XIII century, constructed on top of a former religious building of two centuries before. Over the entrance is an eagle in terracotta by Nicolò dell'Arca. Inside are works by Guercino, Costa and the copy of Santa Cecilia by Raffaello, originally kept here and now at the local art gallery. The bell-tower is of the end of the XV century.

Returning to via Farini, we come into via Santo Stefano, natural continuation of the street, and turn left immediately, going back down the street. We thus find ourselves in the beautiful square which takes its name from the Saint and which the Bolognese also call the **square of the seven churches** as, in the past, seven churches actually stood there. Today, only four remain; the church of the Crucifix, of the Holy Sepulchre, of the Trinity and of saints Vitale and Agricola. This complex, in Romanesque style, is built around a primitive construction, that of the Holy Sepulchre, which goes back to the V century, and is attributed to the XI and XIII centuries. However, also the church of saints Vitale and Agricola, which was reconstructed for the last time in the XI century, was perhaps begun in the IV century and some say it was Bologna's first cathedral. The exceptionally bare and austere interior is decorated by beautiful capitals and traces of partly destroyed frescoes.

On leaving the church, note the surrounding houses and palazzos, among which are the **Bolognini palazzos**, one of which has a façade decorated with almost 200 terracotta heads.

1. Palazzo Ruini Ranuzzi, now the Palace of Justice, by Palladio (16th C). 2. Minghetti square, with the monument dedicated to the politician (by Giulio Monteverde). 3. Church of S. Giovanni in Monte: the 1474 façade. 4. St. John's eagle, a magnificent terracotta work by Nicolò dell'Arca.

Continue along via Santo Stefano as far as the curious XIII century shop (obviously the oldest in the city). The **Seracchioli and Reggiani houses** can be seen here.

We thus arrive in **piazza della Mercanzia** with the Loggia dei Mercanti (of the Merchants), on the site of the ancient customs house of the Commune. It was built in 1390 and the decisions of the Merchants' Tribunal were red from the balcony. The decorations are

1. Basilica of S. Stefano, or «Holy Jerusalem» compound. 2. Church of San Vitale and Santa Agricola, interior. 3. Church of the Holy Sepulchre, interior. 4. The crypt of the Abbot Martino.

3

4

33

34

St. Stephen's Basilica: 1. Church of the Holy Trinity, interior. 2. Manger by Simone dei Crocifissi, polychromatic wood (14th C). 3. Pilate's Niche, located in the center of the courtyard of the same name. 4. The beautiful cloister with two rows of galleries (10th-13th C). 5. Stone well, with curb and delta dating from 1632. 6. The Romanesque belltower, unique of all the «seven churches».

1

2

in brickwork, by various artists. It was constructed by Lorenzo di Bagnomarino and Antonio di Vincenzo. It has

suffered some damage during the course of the centuries: the last occasion being during the second war. It now houses the Chamber of Commerce. From the square and facing the Loggia, we make a brief detour to the right along via Castiglione, to admire the **Pepoli palazzos** of the XIV century, and in front of us, Pepoli Campogrande palazzo, partly rebuilt in the XII century. Inside are several valuable frescoes among which are some by Donato Creti. We now return to Piazza della Mercanzia and then, going straight ahead, we find ourselves at the foot of the beautiful symbol of the city, the **Two Towers**. The highest is the Asinelli tower, being 97,20 metres high, and it was begun in 1109. It has an incline of approximately $2^1/_2$ metres. The top can be reached by climbing the long flights of stairs inside, which, through tiring, permit you to admire a stupendous view not only of the city, but of most of the province too. In the XIV century, it was used as a prison. The battlemented open gallery is of the XV century. The Garisenda tower is 47 metres high and has an incline of 3.20

36

3

metres. It was built in more of less the same period as the Asinelli tower, then considerably lowered two and a half centuries later, for safety reasons. Its original height is not known.

Right next to the Two Towers is the **church of San Bartolomeo**, built around the mid 1600's. Inside is a Madonna with Child by Guido Reni and several valuable frescoes.

St. Dominic's Basilica: 1. Simone dei Crocifissi: triptych of the Saints Abbot Benedict, Pope Sistus and Proculus Martyr. 2. Marco Berlinghieri: the Slaughter of the Innocents, detail (13th C). 3. Palazzo Bolognini. 4. Seracchioli buildings and Alberici Tower (13th C).

4

37

38

3
1. The elegant Merchants' Palace dates to the 14th century. 2. Via Castiglione: the ancient Palazzo Pepoli (14th C). 3. Via Rizzoli viewed from the West.

39

of the Roman via Emilia. After a walk of a few hundred yards, we come to one of the most characteristic Bolognese palazzos, **casa Isolani**, at no. 19. This represents one of the few remaining examples of XII century houses, in the Gothic-Romanesque style, with wooden «Stylized» porticos. Just a little further ahead, the street suddenly opens out into the impressive **square of Santa Maria dei Servi**, with the characteristic Renaissance porticoed quadran-

Leaving the church, we turn left into **Strada Maggiore**, one of the most characteristic streets of the city, and which forms one of the «civic» tracts

40

gle. Its construction was begun aroung 1350, but it is believed to have been finished almost a century and a half later. The interior is in Gothic style and houses various art treasures: a Virgin by Cimabue and numerous paintings by Francesco Albani, Alessandro Tiarini, Vitale da Bologna, etc. The side which faces Strada Maggiore is also interesting, with the most ancient portion of the Loggia attributed to the architect Antonio da Vincenzo. The farlights preserve XVII century frescoes, depicting the life of S. Filippo Beniti, founder of the Servite order.

1. Basilica of the Saints Bartholomew and Gaetano at the Two Towers (17th-18th C). 2. Casa Isolani (13th C). 3. Basilica of St. Mary of the Servants: the façade with its four-sided portico, completed in the 19th century. 4. Glimpse of the portico: the segment by Antonio di Vincenzo. 5. St. Mary of the Servants: the harmonious interior. 6. Cimabue: Madonna with Child in Dignity (13th C).

41

In front of the church, on the other side of Strada Maggiore and on the corner of the characteristic **piazza Aldrovandi**, which contains one of the most colourful markets of Bologna, is the beautiful **Davia Bargellini palazzo**, now housing the industrial art Museum. It was built in 1600 by Bartolomeo Provaglia. Inside is a notable staircase. The balcony, supported by two gigantic telamones, is typical of the period and from this comes the name «palazzo of the giants» given to it by the older Bolognese.

Walking right across piazza Aldrovandi, we come out into **via San Vitale**, once called «via del sale (salt street), as its natural continuation (today the State road) led to the salt mines of Cervia. Immediately on the left we can admire the «gatetower» of the circle of walls of the XII century. Passing under it, we see immediately on our left the beautiful **Fantuzzi palazzo**, with the characteristic ashlar-work front. It was begun at the beginning of the XVI century by the Fantuzzi family and was finished around 1600. It is uncertain who was the author of the building: some say it was realized by Triachini while others consider it the work of Formigine.

Continuing along via San Vitale we come back to the Two Towers again, from which we can begin the 2nd itinerary.

Basilica of St. Mary of the Servants: 1. Vitale da Bologna: Madonna of the Birth (14th C). 2. The «portal of the giants» of the aerial portico of the Servants. 3. Via San Vitale: Palazzo Fantuzzi (16th C). 4. Piazza Ravegnana: the Drapers Palace (15th C).

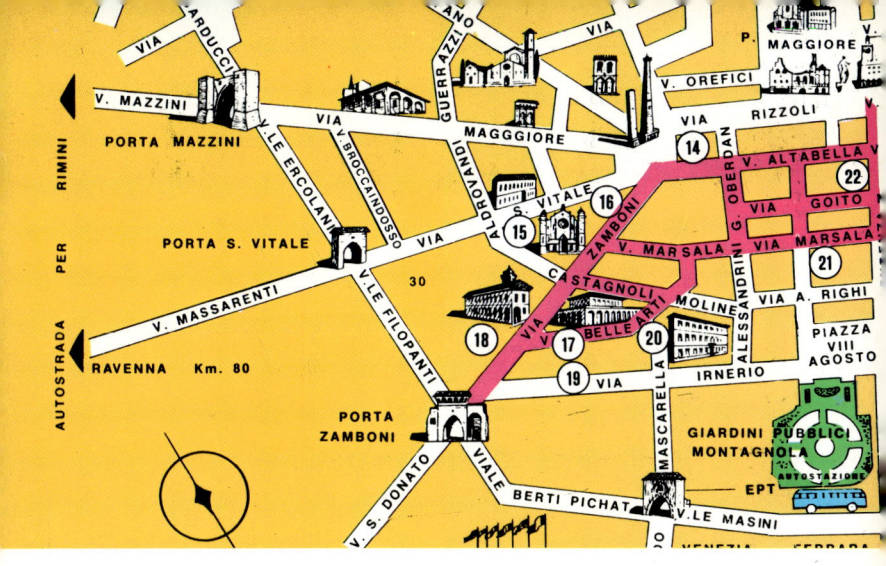

2nd Itinerary

Summary:

14 Drapers' Palace
15 G.B. Martini Conservatory of Music
16 Church of St. James the Elder
17 Community Theatre
18 University Palace
19 National Art Gallery
20 Palazzo Bentivoglio
21 Palazzo Grassi
22 Saint Peter's Metropolitan

In front of us is the **palazzo dei Drappieri** (Linen Drapers), sometimes known as the «Strazzaroli» (Rag Merchants), built at the end of the XV century to house the corporation of this trade. On our right is the start of via Zamboni, once called via San Donato, from the church dedicated to this Saint, standing a few hundred yards further on and built in the XV century with successive modifications. In this street stand some of the most beautiful Bolognese palazzos: **palazzo Malvasia**, with its fine neoclassical façade of the XVIII century, **palazzo Malvezzi de' Medici**, now the seat of the provincial Administration, designed by Triachini in the XVI century, **palazzo Malvezzi-Campeggi**, by Formigine, built in the XVI century etc. Walking alongside the provincial Administration palazzo, we come to the house where the famous Cardinal Lambertini was born, later to become Pope Benedict XIV.

But there are other beautiful buildings facing onto the square. **Palazzo Magnani**, next to Malvezzi, by Tibaldi and built towards the end of the XVI century; the «**G. B. Martini**» conservatory of music, housed in the ex-Agostinian convent, and the beautiful **church of San Giacomo Maggiore**. Before beginning the visit to the church, to which particular attention should be paid, we should remember that in the Martini conservatory there is the Civic Bibliographic Museum of Music, one of the most complete in Europe. Alongside portraits and autographs of musicians are antique music scores, early musical instruments and other valuable curiosities. It should be noted that some of the most famous names in music of various periods, lived in the conservatory as teachers of pupils: Busoni, Martucci, Rossini, Donizetti, etc. And now we are ready to begin the visit to San Giacomo. First of all, the XIII century façade with the statue of the Saint should be noted.

The interior immediately presents evidence of the successive modifications. The nave is unique and Renaissance in style. There are numerous chapels and 34 altars. It is almost impossible to describe all the works of art housed here: frescoes, paintings, altarpieces, statues and crucifixes all carry evidence of Italian Masters. Among them are Ludovico Carracci (the San Rocco), Francesco Francia (the altarpiece with the enthroned Virgin), Bartolomeo Passarotti (the Madonna with

1. Palazzo Malvezzi de' Medici, by Triachini (16th C). 2. Conservatory of music: the ancient portal of the Augustinians. 3. Bossi Hall, with part of the Picture Gallery of Father Martini. 4. St. James the Elder: façade from 1295. 5. St. James the Elder: the peaceful Renaissance interior.

Saints), Jacopo di Paolo (polyptych), Simone dei Crocifissi (Crucifix), il Bagnacavallo, Lorenzo Costa, Jacopo della Quercia, etc. Among the chapels, that of the Bentivoglios, is particularly interesting, with a painting by Francia,

45

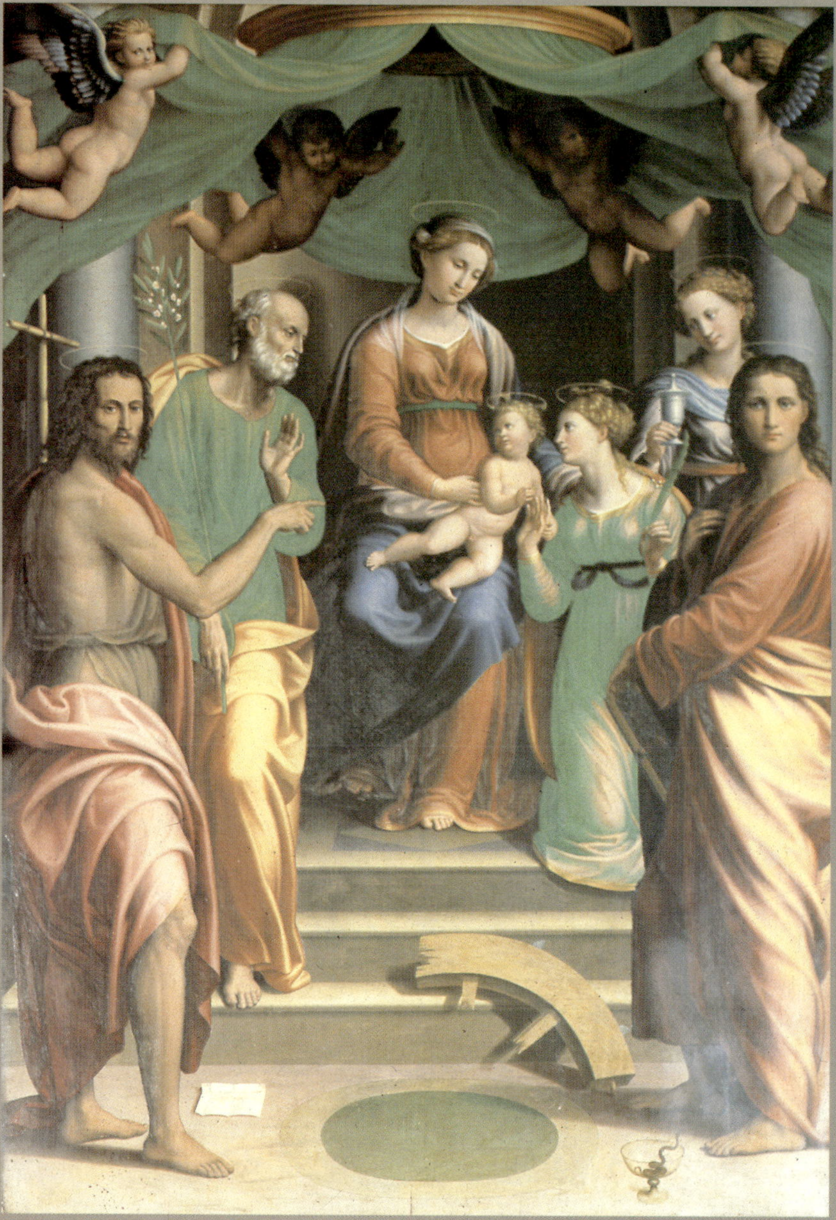

alto-rilievo by Nicolò dell'Arca and other valuable works. The numerous funeral monuments inside the church should also be noted.

On leaving the church, the splendid portico formed by 36 Corinthian columns with capitals, each one different from the others, should be admired. Under the portico are the Gothic

St. James the Elder: 1. Innocenzo da Imola: the mystical marriage of St. Catherine. 2. Jacopo della Quercia: arc of Antonio Galeazzi Bentivogli. 3. Jacopo di Paolo: Polyptych of the incoronation of Mary. 4. Simone dei Crocifissi: Crucifix from 1370. 5. Francesco Raibolino, known as Francia: Mary with Child and Saints.

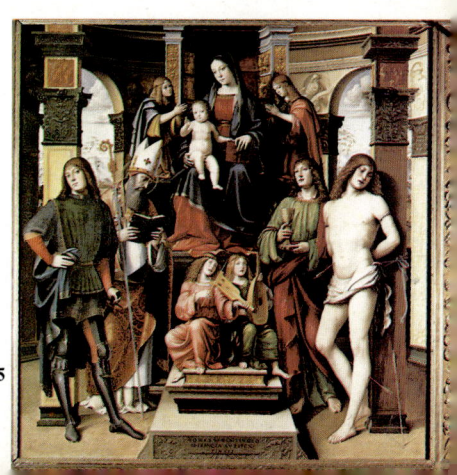

«arches» with some traces of the original frescoes which decorated them.

Continuing, on our right we see the convent of San Giacomo and the little **church-oratory of Santa Cecilia**, with frescoes of the life of the Saint by Francia, Lorenzo Costa and others.

Further ahead is **piazza Verdi**, on the right-hand side of which, a part of the ancient XII century wall can be noted. On the left-hand side is the **Communal Theatre** by Bibiena. Its history is long and complex. Originally the Malvezzi theatre, wellpatronized by the Bolognese, always lovers of good music, it was built on the ruins of the Bentivoglio palazzo, at one time the most beautiful of the city. One unfortunate day in February 1745, however, a fire «stole» this place of delight and the city was left without its musical temple. It took the intervention of Cardinal Lambertini to make a group of Bolognese agree to reconstruct a new theatre and it was thus decided to entrust the project to the Bolognese architect then in favour, for the construction of theatres and places of entertainment, Antonio Galli, known as il Bibiena. And it was in his own city, after having designed theatres in various parts of Europe, that he expressed the best of his abilities. For the inauguration of the theatre, he even wanted to contribute to the scenography and to the costumes for the chosen opera: «The triumph of Clelia», music by Gluck, libretto by Metastasio. From then on, the Bologna Communal Theatre had some of the most famous names in the world of classical, lyrical and symphonic entertainment, as its guests. It was here that Toscanini began his climb to success. The present aspect of the theatre differs little from that of the original: struck by a fire in 1931, it was damaged but restored within the course of three years.

Leaving the «Comunale» we continue along via Zamboni. A few yards ahead, on the right, is the famous **University**, the ancient Bolognese Studio. Established in the XVI century palazzo Poggi, designed by Pellegrino

1. St. Cecilia's Church: Baptism of Valeriano, attributed to Giacomo and Guido Francia. 2. Lorenzo Costa: Conversion of Valeriano. 3. Community Theatre, inaugurated in 1763. In Piazza Verdi, in front of the theatre, three sculptures by Arnaldo Pomodoro. 4. Community Theatre: BIBIENA hall.

Tibaldi, it has housed the university for two and a half centuries. It was in fact in about 1710 when, in the palazzo built for Cardinal Giovanni Poggi, the Institute of Science was established here, on the wishes of Luigi Ferdinando Marsigli. Next to this and soon after came the Benedictine Academy, now the Academy of Science, and the museum donated by the same Marsigli. It was not until the beginning of the next century that the other specializations, formerly housed in the Archiginnasio palazzo, were also transferred here. New buildings were then needed, those of the palazzo Poggi being insufficient, and so the nearby Malvezzi palazzo was acquired for the «Studio». In the court-

49

yard of the University is a beautiful statue by Angelo Piò, depicting Hercules. Inside are frescoes by Tibaldi, and busts and memorial stones which commemorate the most illustrious lecturers and students. Of particular interest is the library, whose reading room, requested by Cardinal Lambertini, was designed by Dotti. The observatory tower on top of the building is also interesting: built in 1725 based on a project by Giuseppe Antonio Torri, it houses the University astronomical observatory.

On leaving the University, we continue for a few yards more along via Zamboni. Arriving in sight of the ancient Gate of the last circle of walls, we find ourselves at the junction of several roads. The one on the left is via Belle Arti. Here, at no. 56, is the **National Art Gallery**, housed in the ex Jesuit convent of Sant'Ignazio. This is one of the most beautiful art collections existing in Italy for the wealth of art works by some of the most famous artists. One of the sections, the one dedicated to the 1300's, is second only to the Uffizi Gallery in Florence. To visit it thoroughly, one has to walk round almost 3,000 metres of exhibits. We will note at least a part of the most well-known names whose works are gathered here: from Giotto and several of his school to Raffaello, from Domenichino to Reni, from Cima da Conegliano to Parmigianino, from Crespi to Perugino, and then naturally, Carracci, Tiziano, Veronese, Tintoretto, and a group of artists who go under the name of «Primitives» and who in this case too, place the Bolognese collection among the first in Europe. Next to the Art Gallery, is a collection of prints and drawings with almost 5,000 works. Leaving the Art

1. Palazzo Poggi, administration building of the University: the magnificent courtyard. 2. The Speculum Tower (18th C) rises above the university city. 3. National Art Gallery, Vitale da Bologna: St. George and the Dragon.

51

Gallery, not without regret, let us continue along via Belle Arti as far as the **new Palazzo Bentivoglio**. Majestic and impressive, it was built towards the end of the 1500's. The interior courtyard is particularly interesting. It is incomplete

1. National Art Gallery. The Crucifix of St. Mary of the Burg (18th C). 2. Vitale da Bologna: tablet with two stories of St. Anthony Abbot. 3. Ludovico Carracci: Madonna Bargellini. 4. Donato Creti: Achille diving into the River Styx. 5. Jacopo di Francesco: Polyptych. 6. Hall of frescoes by Mezzaratta.

52

5

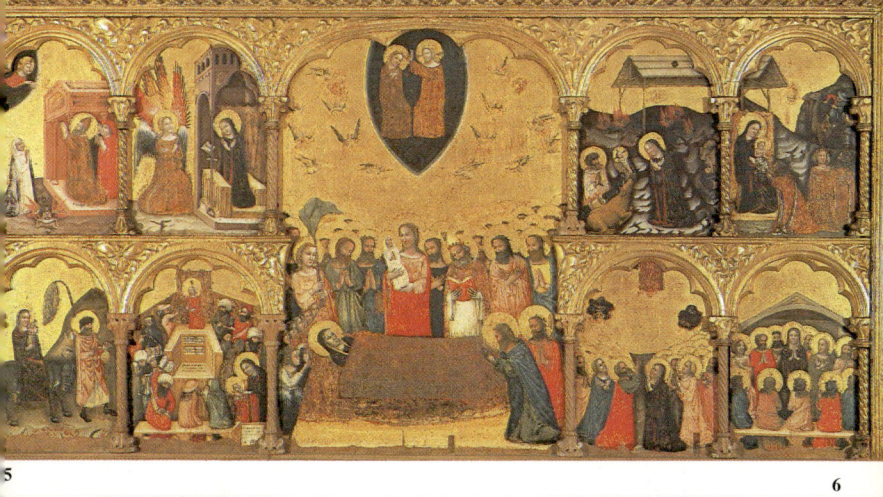

6

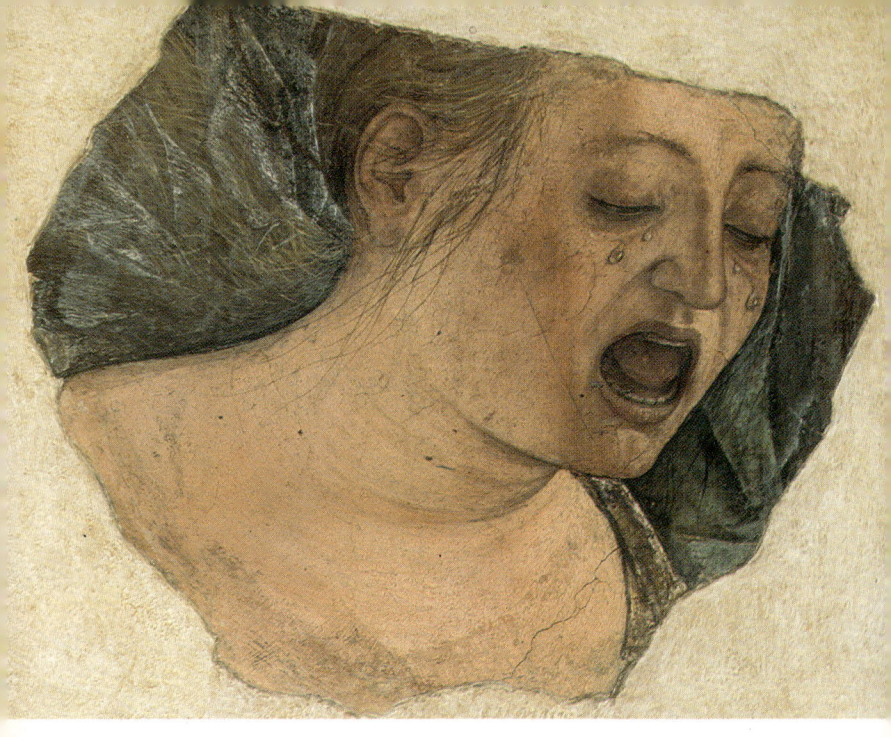

1. National Art Museum. Ercole Roberti: fragment with the weeping Madonna. 2. Domenico Theotocopulos, known as El Greco: last Supper. 3. Guido Reni: Slaughter of the Innocents.

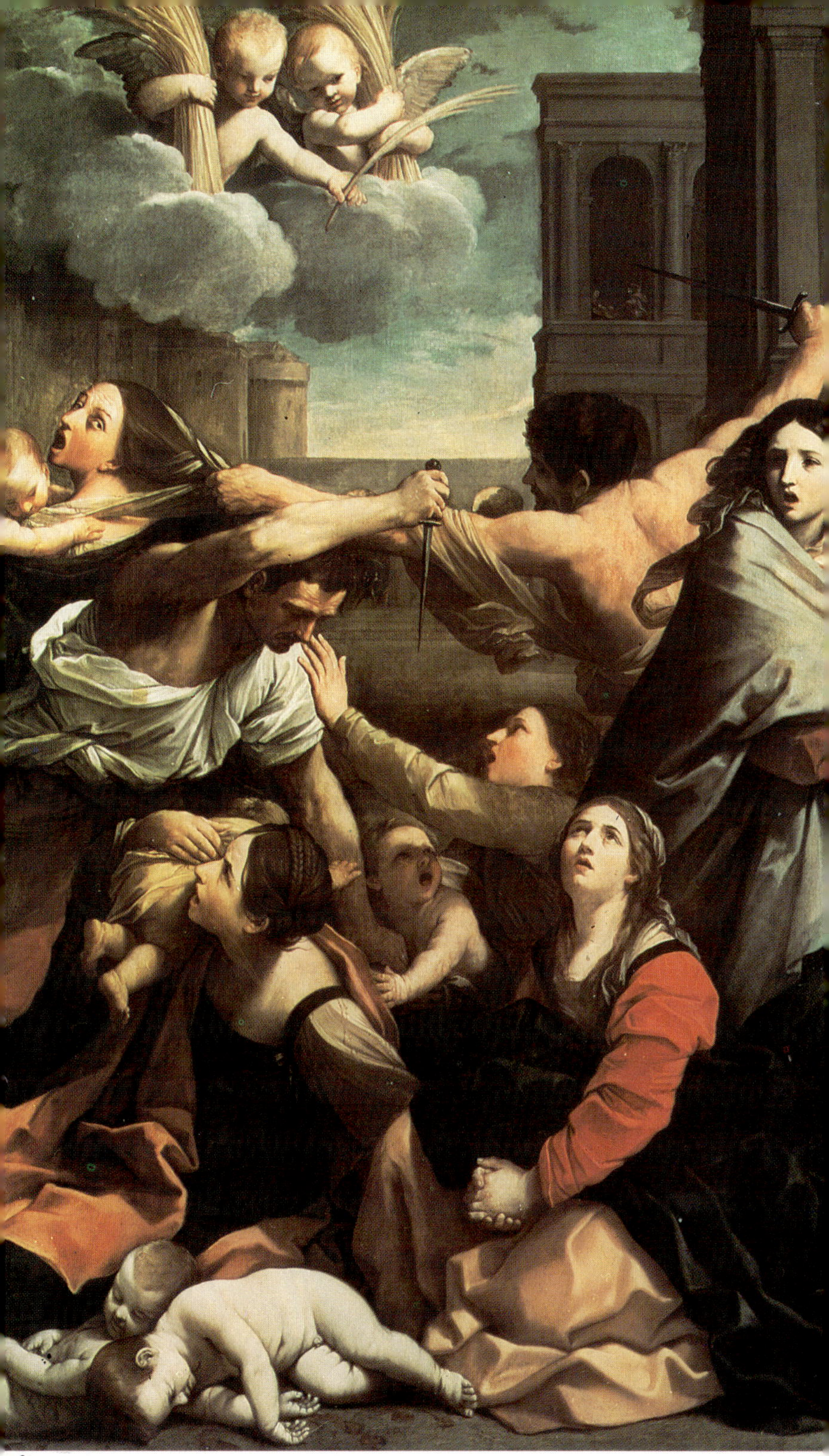

3

1. *National Art Museum. Giovanni Francesco Barbieri, known as Guercino (the Squinter): St. Sebastian being cared for by Irene.* 2. *Francesco la Cossa: the Merchants' Alterpiece. 3. Raffaello Sanzio: Ecstasy of St. Cecilia.*

3

and was realized by Falcetti around 1625.

Almost in front of the Palazzo Bentivoglio, via Castagnoli begins, and by walking along this street we come along the side of the Communal Theatre and so back into via Zamboni. Here we turn right until we reach the junction with the antique via Marsala, practically in front of the portico of San Giacomo Maggiore. By walking along via Marsala for about 200 yards, we come to **piazza San Martino**, where there is a church dedicated to this Saint. It is very old (it is a said to have been founded by the Carmelites at the beginning of the 1400's) and its interior is subdivided into three naves, with numerous chapels, some of which have particular artistic interest. Frescoes by Bigari, Tiarini, paintings by Francia and a beautiful stained glass window by de Beauvais, decorate the interior. Above the entrance, facing onto via Marsala, there is an alto-rilievo which commemorates the gift of the Saint's cloak to the poor, by Manzini. The organ, built in the XVI century, is interesting. In the square is a column with the Madonna of Carmine by Ferreri.

Continuing along via Marsala, after passing the crossroads, we reach one of the oldest Bolognese palazzos, the **Palazzo Grassi**, now housing the Officers' Club. Together with the «casa Isolani» which we saw in the preceding itinerary, it holds «first place» for antiquity: it was in fact built in the XIII century and is a beautiful example of Romanesque-Gothic style. The wooden styled portico and the big pointed arch door are particularly effective. The single-slit windows are decorated with terracottas.

Further along via Marsala, we come out into via Indipendenza and, turning left we go along for a few yards and turn left again into via Goito, parallel to via Marsala. Here is a beautiful XVI century palazzo, **Palazzo Bocchi**, built

1. Palazzo Bentivoglio (16th C). 2. St. Martin's Basilica: the façade dating from 1879. 3. The harmonious Gothic interior (14th-15th C).

2

3

59

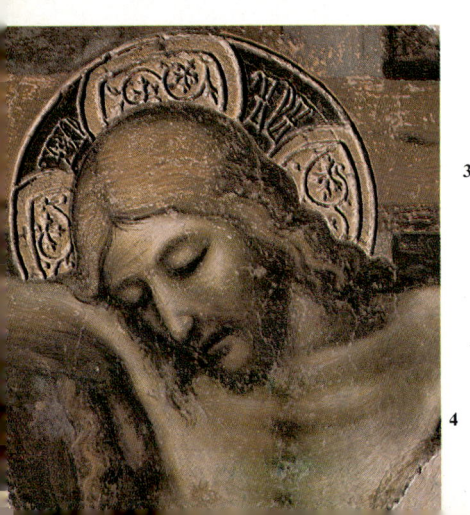

on the design by Vignola and then modified by Mascherino. Several latin and hebrew verses are sculpted on the base. Turning back into via Indipendenza and continuing along this street, we find the Palazzo del Monte di Pietà on our left and in the same street is the **house of Pope Gregory XIII**, reformer of the calendar, **Palazzo Boncompagni**, from the name of his family. The courtyard and the beautiful frescoes inside are interesting. On the main door is the coat-of-arms of Pope Ugo Boncompagni.

And so we arrive at the Metropolitan **church of San Pietro**, whose cannons, in the past, occupied the present-day Palazzo del Monte. The origins of this beautiful church, which is the Bolognese Cathedral, go back to the X century (shortly after the beginning) but it has undergone numerous and even relatively recent modifications. It was semi-destroyed by the earthquake in the XII century but even before that, about one century, it was struck by the terrible fire which struck the city and restored, ornamented and modified several times. It carries interesting evidence of all these modifications, like the lions which offer holy water to the faithful, the spiral column of the Baptistry, the bell tower containing the

1. St. Martin's Basilica. Paolo Uccello: Christ's Nativity. 2. San Rocco, stained glass by Giacomo da Ulma based on a drawing by Francia. 3. Francia: Madonna with Child and Saints. 4. Vitale da Bologna: fragment of fresco with Crucifix. 5. The wooden portico (13th C) of Palazzo Grassi. 6. St. Peter's Cathedral: the façade (18th C).

61

original paleo-Romanesque bell «swallowed up» by its costruction, the Romanesque cedar-wood Crucifix, etc. The ancient doorway is beautiful and impressive, facing onto the side street via Altabella. Inside the church are works of importance: by Creti, Ludovico Carracci, Alfonso Lombardi, etc. The crypt by Tibaldi holds relics of Saints Vitale and Agricola, which come from the church of Santo Stefano. At this point we advise leaving the church by the side entrance, thus coming out into via Altabella. Here we can see the beautiful **tower of the Azzoguidis**, of the XII century. Not far from here, in via Sant'Alò, is another tower, that of the **Prendiparte**, built in the same period. The latter is a metre less in height than the former (59 metres) and has the nickname of «Coronata» (crowned) be cause of the teeth of the offset. It also served as a prison. From via Altabella, crossing via Caduti di Cefalonia, we come back into via Rizzoli and again into the shadow of the Two Towers, where the second itinerary finishes.

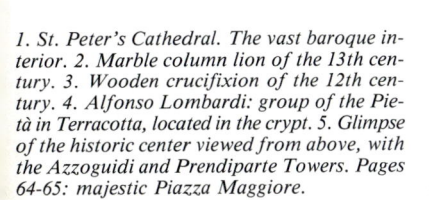

1. St. Peter's Cathedral. The vast baroque interior. 2. Marble column lion of the 13th century. 3. Wooden crucifixion of the 12th century. 4. Alfonso Lombardi: group of the Pietà in Terracotta, located in the crypt. 5. Glimpse of the historic center viewed from above, with the Azzoguidi and Prendiparte Towers. Pages 64-65: majestic Piazza Maggiore.

63

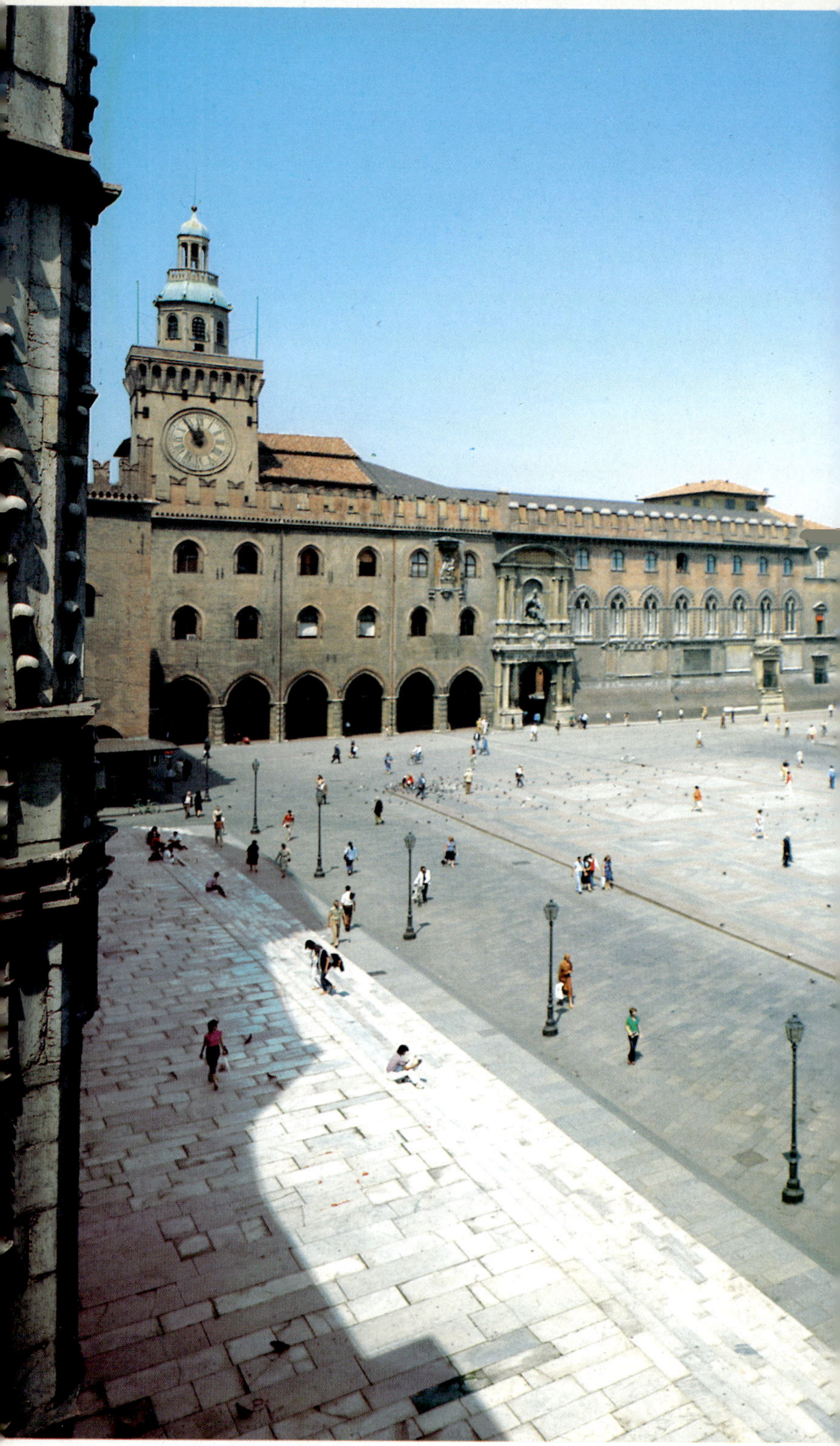

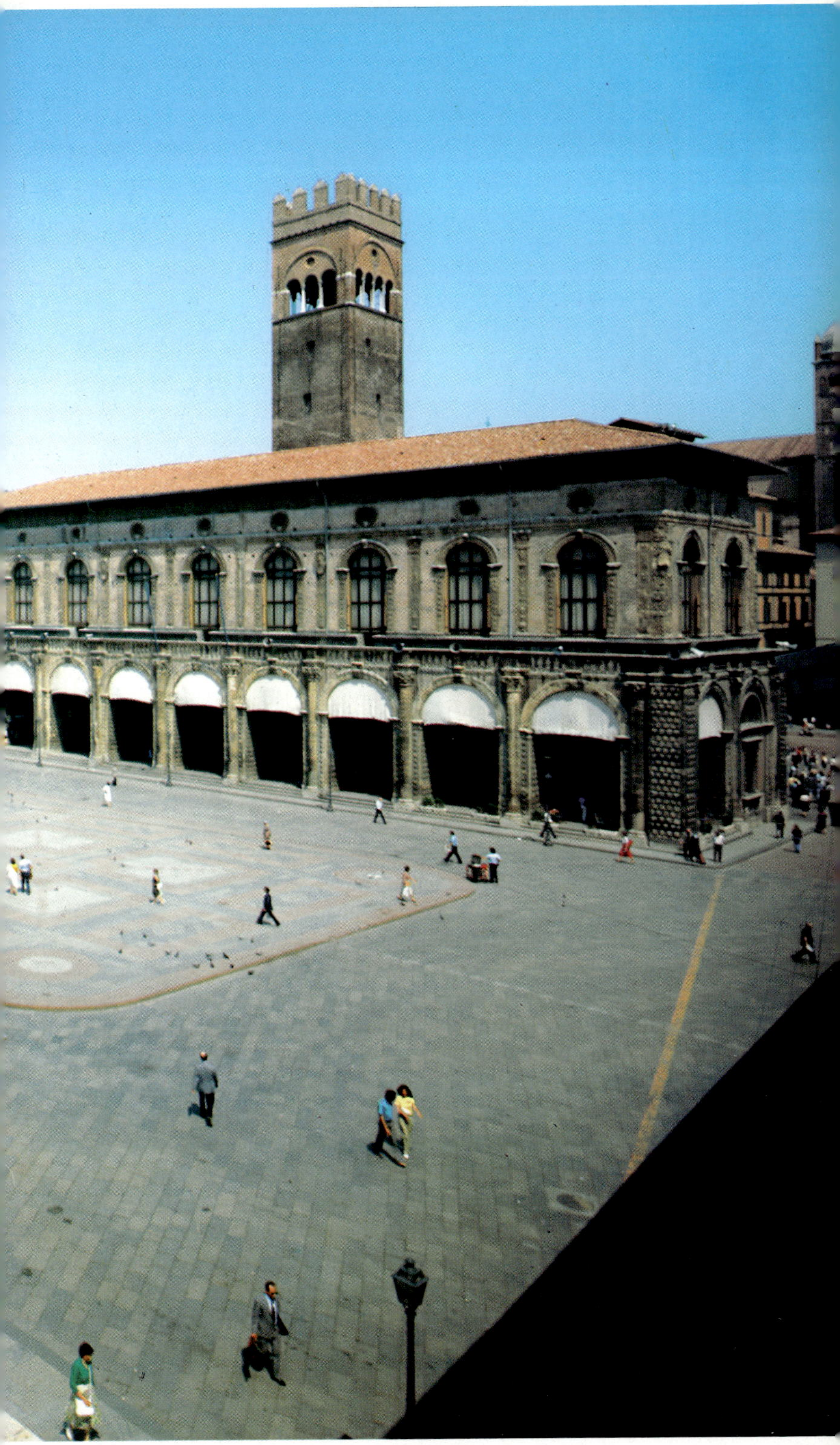

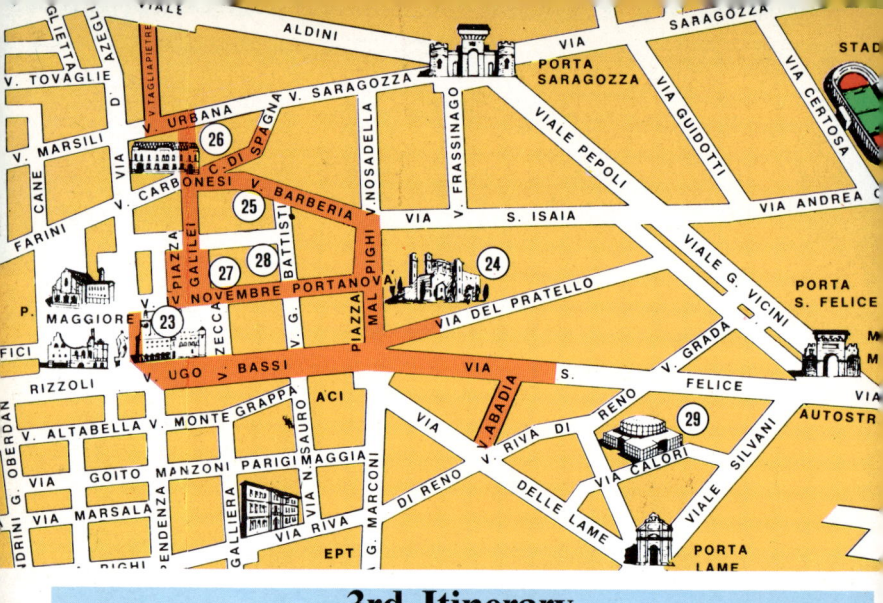

3rd Itinerary

Summary:

23 Palazzo d'Accursio and Community Art Collections
24 Saint Francis' Church
25 National Tapestry Museum
26 Palazzo Bevilacqua
27 Palazzo Caprara
28 Church of San Salvatore and Palazzo Marescalchi
29 Palazzo dello Sport

Still taking the junction of via Rizzoli and Ugo Bassi with piazza Nettuno and via Indipendenza as a reference point, and keeping the previously admired palazzo Re Enzo and Neptune's fountain on our left, let us walk along past the Sanctuary to the War Dead and we thus arrive at the main entrance to the **Palazzo d'Accursio**, seat of the Town Hall. A curious ensemble, bearing traces of various styles, it appears almost like a fortress just having been refined by the mullioned windows and by the statue of Gregory XIII, as well as by the Madonna by Nicolò dell'Arca, «set» into its façade.

Its construction began in the XIII century, for the jurist Accursio. The tower, then raised, containing the clock of Gandolfi, is of the period. The right-hand part, where the mullioned windows are found, is of the XV century. The main entrance is probably of the mid XVI century and the bronze statue of Pope Boncompagni is from the end of the same century.

1. Piazza Maggiore is bordered on the west by the block of the Civic Palace. 2. Palazzo d'Accursio. 3. The large window by Alessi (1555).

67

1. Palazzo d'Accursio. The Portal by Galeazzo Alessi (16th C). 2. Gregory XIII, bronze by Alessandro Menganti (1580). 3. La Madonna di Piazza, terracotta by Nicolò dell'Arca.

1. Palazzo d'Accursio. The Court of Honour (15th C). Copy (1934) of the sixteenth-century cistern by Terribilia. 3. Stone stairway attributed to Bramante.

The two courtyards are particularly interesting: the first, which faces onto piazza Maggiore, is by Fioravanti and was constructed at the beginning of the XV century; the second is more recent but equally impressive, this time due to its width and perspectives. At the centre is the cistern copied from the original by Terribilia. The wide staircase leading to the upper floors is also interesting. Each step in fact has a stone cordon, now worn away and very smooth: it was used to allow the horses to reach the upper rooms. And speaking of rooms, the splendid Farnese and Ercole chambers should be visited. These contain a gigantic statue and remains of frescoes by Bibiena and Cignani. Visit also the chambers of the communal art

1. Palazzo d'Accursio. Hall of the City Council, with sixteenth-century frescoes. 2. The city banner, decorated with two gold medals. 3. Community Art Collections: Francesco Francia: Crucifixion. 4. Donato Creti: Mercury and Paris. 5. Luca Signorelli: Head of a Saint.

3
4
5
6

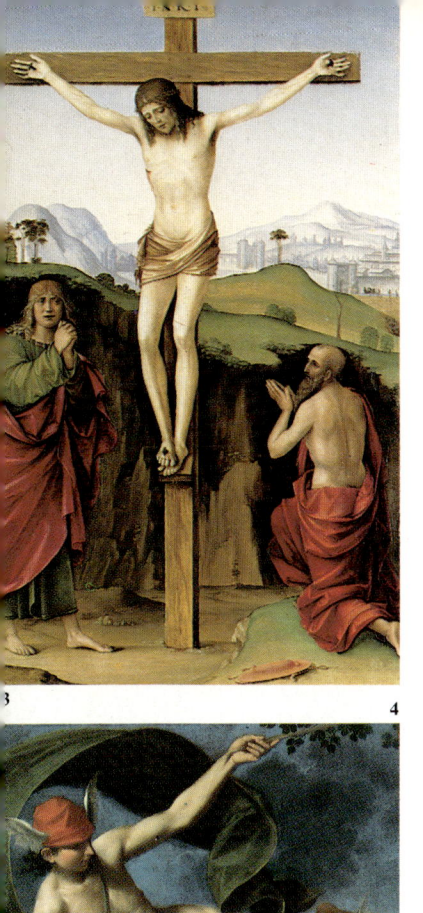

collection, which were used for the apartment of the Pontifical Legate at the time when the city had a Papal Regency.

Among the works of art on display, some of which are simple furnishings but of great artistic or artisan value, we should note the clocks, silver, ceramics, crystal, miniatures as well as a certain number of pieces of furniture. Among the paintings are works by Simone dei Crocifissi, Francesco Francia, Tintoretto, Signorelli, Hayez, etc.

We can now leave by the door which faces onto via Ugo Bassi. Continuing along this street for about 400 metres and keeping to the left, we come to the junction with piazza Malpighi. Before turning left into the square, we can pause to admire the palazzetto in front of us and which is known as the «Ospedaletto», built in 1585 and designed by Domenico Tibaldi.

On our left, opens the beautiful **piazza Malpighi**, in the centre of which is the column with the statue of the Madonna. It was erected in 1638 and

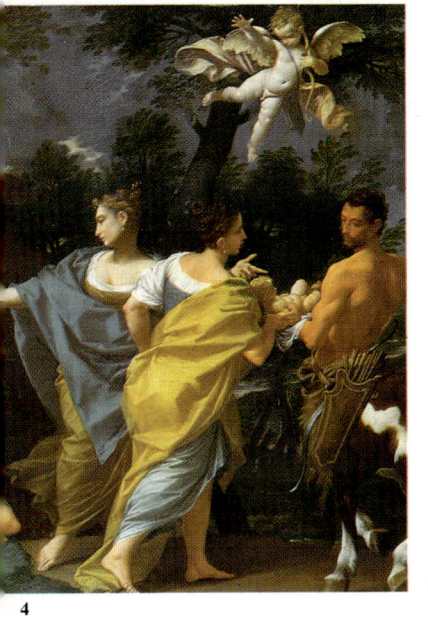

1. Community Art Collections: Ubaldo: Diana and Hendimone. 2. Amico Aspertini: Madonna with Child (16th C). 3. 14th-century Tuscan school: Redeemer. 4. Donato Creti: Achille. 5. G. Maria Crespi: Cardinal Lambertini (sketch). 6. Bolognese school (17th C): Madonna with Child. 7. Francesco Hayez: Ruth (19th C).

the Madonna, in copper, is by Guido Reni. On the 8th of December, at the foot of the image, «la fiorita», a rite of homage to the Madonna is celebrated with the participation of the local population.

On the right of the square we have the imposing bulk of the **church of San Francesco**. This is one of the most ancient examples of Franciscan churches: it was in fact erected between 1235 and 1236. It is said that some years before its construction was begun (in 1222) the Saint came to preach in Bologna, in the nearby piazza Maggiore. It is uncertain who designed it, but the French influence is certainly present. We must mention the names of Marco di Brescia and of his brother friar Giovanni and of another friar who was probably the «maestro» of the church: friar Andrea. The interior has the form of the latin cross with three naves. The one in

1. *Piazza Malpighi and St. Francis' Basilica.*
2. *Piazza San Francesco: Madonna by Reni.*
3. *San Francis' Basilica; the façade (13th C).*
4. *The central nave.*

the middle, the highest, has vaults with six sections, like Notre-Dame in Paris. The Romanesque-Gothic façade is decorated with marble panels and majolica basins. There are two belltowers: the smallest, going back to the construction of the church, was completed by a spire which was demolished in the XVIII century. The higher tower, of the beginning of the XV century, was designed by maestro Antonio di Vincenzo and recalls, by its form, the

75

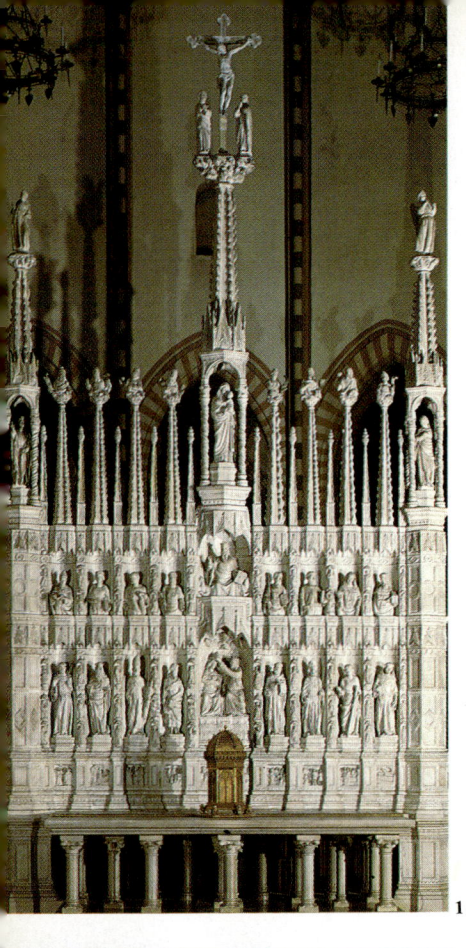

Florentine bell-tower of Santa Maria del Fiore.

Also worth noting are the beautiful rampant arches which run around the exterior of the apse and the entrance next to the bell-tower with tombs and memorial stones. The interior, very impressive and luminous, is also particularly worth admiring. There are nine chapels and a beautiful main altar, with a marble altar-piece by two famous Venetian artists, Jacobello and Pier Paolo delle Masegne, once covered in gold.

There is an interesting XV century chapel to San Bernardino, decorated with terracottas. Inside, in the left-hand side nave, is the brickwork sepulchre of the antipope Alexander V, who died in 1410. At the end of that century, the tomb was completed by Sperandio. The sacristy and the mayor bell-tower are again by majstro Antonio di Vincenzo.

1. St. Francis' Basilica; piece of the main altar by Dalle Masegne. 2. Tomb of the glossators. 3. Sperandio da Mantova and Pietro Lamberti; sepulchre of Pope Alexander Filargo V. 4. The cloister of the dead (late 19th C).

4

The beautiful church was unfortunately damaged quite badly during the last war. Careful restoration work has managed to restore its dignity. Piazza Malpighi contains the impressive **tombs of the Glossators**, or rather commentators of the law: the jurist Accursio and his son Francesco, of 1260, in the barest and most classical sepulchre; of Odofredo, in the one with the double row of columns, and of Rolandino de' Romanzi, in the one with the lions on the corners. Continuing across the square and keeping the church of San Francesco on the right, we come to the palazzo which now houses the financial offices and which was once the convent of the Franciscans. The beautiful arcade, built in the XVII century, is decorated with frescoes on the life of Sant'Antonio da Padova. At the end of this arcade, we find ourselves at a junction: on the left is via Barberia where, after a short walk, we come to the **palazzo Marescotti-Calvi**, now the seat of the Communist Party, with a staircase by the architect Gian Giacomo Monti. Continuing along this street we come to a small square, on the right of which is the **church of San Paolo Maggiore** with a beautiful XVII century faąde. Inside are works by great masters: Ludovico Carracci, il Guercino, l'Algardi, author of the «decollation of San Paolo» which decorates the main altar, and the two Rollis. The Church, built by architect Mazenta in the XVII century, is an elegant example of the baroque style. Among the works of art is a Madonna from the school of Francia.

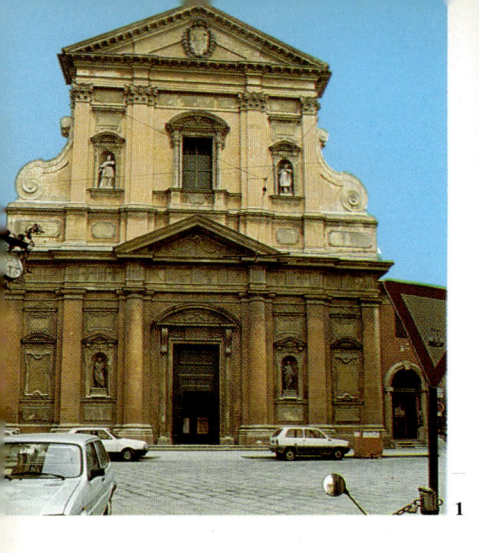

Looking at the faąde of San Paolo, in the street to the right we can see the famous **Spanish College**, which gives its name to the street and which forms an Iberian island in the city, fortress of the privileges conceded to its battlemented walls. The College, the only one left of the many once existing in Bologna, was founded on the request of the Spanish

1. Church of St. Paul the Elder. 2. Cervantes House of the College of Spain: portal by Formigine. 3. The double gallery and wells, with the view of the bell-tower of the Church of St. Clement of the Spaniards. 4. St. Clement's of the Spaniards: interior. 5. Church of the Corpus Domini (15th-17th C). 6. Marcantonio Franceschini: the death of St. Joseph.

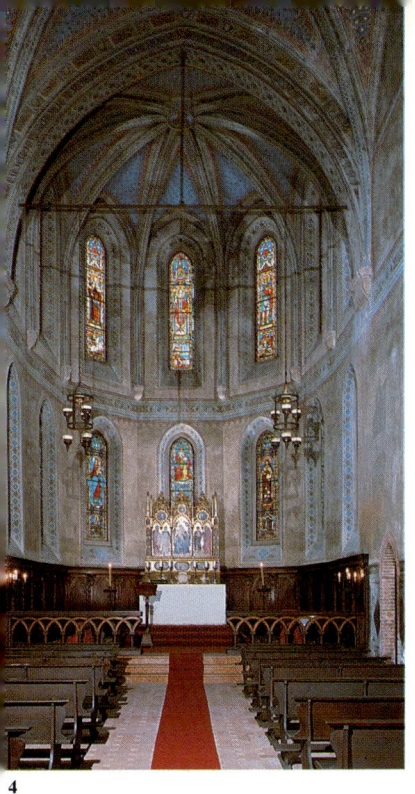

Cardinal Egidio Albornoz, who in this way intended to supply the young nobles attending the Bolognese «studio» with a «home». In reality, more than a home, we must almost call it a fort due to its external aspect. Built in 1367 in typical Renaissance architectural style (even if «seasoned» with Spanish motifs) it is attributed to Matteo Gattaponi. It contains many elements however, due to the other masters of the period: the main door, for example, is said to be by Formigine, while inside, other «hands» can perhaps be distinguished. Particularly effective is the double open gallery of the courtyard, with the two wells. This open gallery is repeated in the building facing onto the garden. Also of interest is the **church of San Clemente of the Spaniards**, in the Gothic style, with the altar-piece by Marco Zoppo depicting the Virgin and Saints.

Inside the «College» is a notable library, housing, amongst other things, precious antique codices.

Returning to the church of San Paolo Maggiore, we have via Tagliapietre on our left. Walking along the side of the church and passing a crossroads, we come to the **church of Corpus Domini**, also known as the church «of the Saint» as it houses the uncorrupted body of Santa Caterina de' Vigri. The XV century church was initially con-

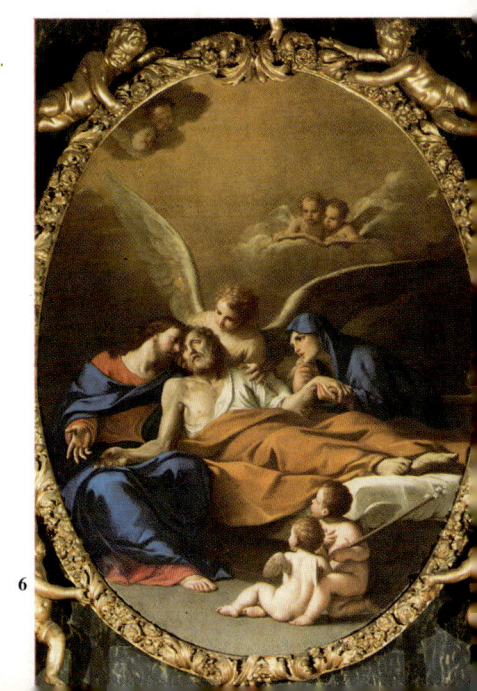

80

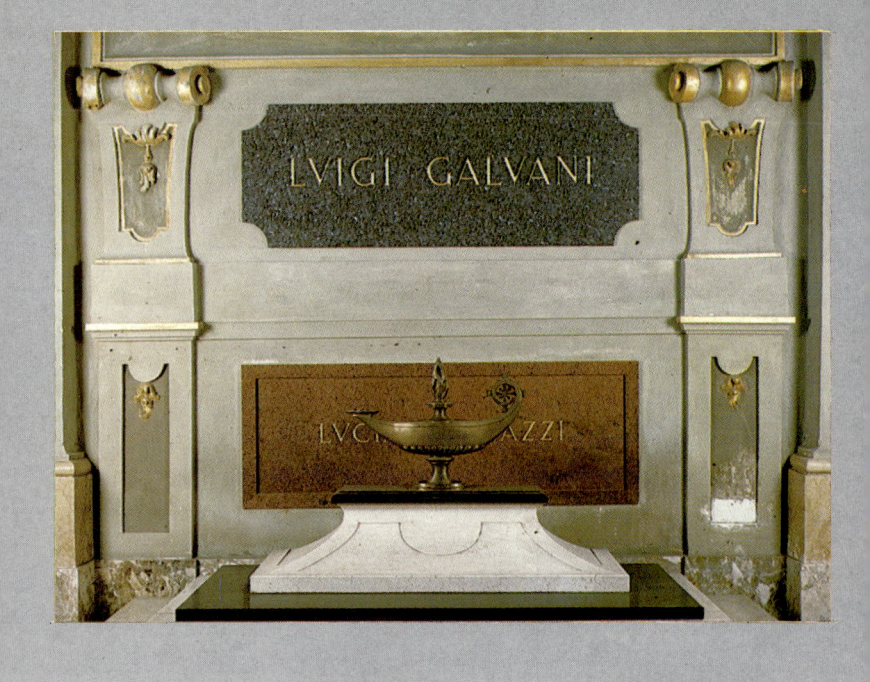

structed for the convent of Santa Maria delle Muratelle. Caterina de' Vigri came here in the mid 1400's to found a monastery of the Poor Clares. The little chapel of Santa Maria delle Muratelle already existed on this site. The façde is Renaissance in style and is decorated with brickwork ornamentations, perhaps by Sperandio.

Inside the church is also the tomb of the great scientist Luigi Galvani and that of Laura Bassi.

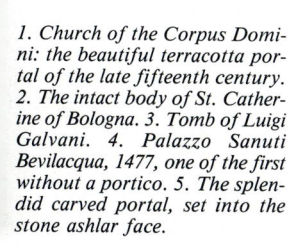

1. Church of the Corpus Domini: the beautiful terracotta portal of the late fifteenth century. 2. The intact body of St. Catherine of Bologna. 3. Tomb of Luigi Galvani. 4. Palazzo Sanuti Bevilacqua, 1477, one of the first without a portico. 5. The splendid carved portal, set into the stone ashlar face.

81

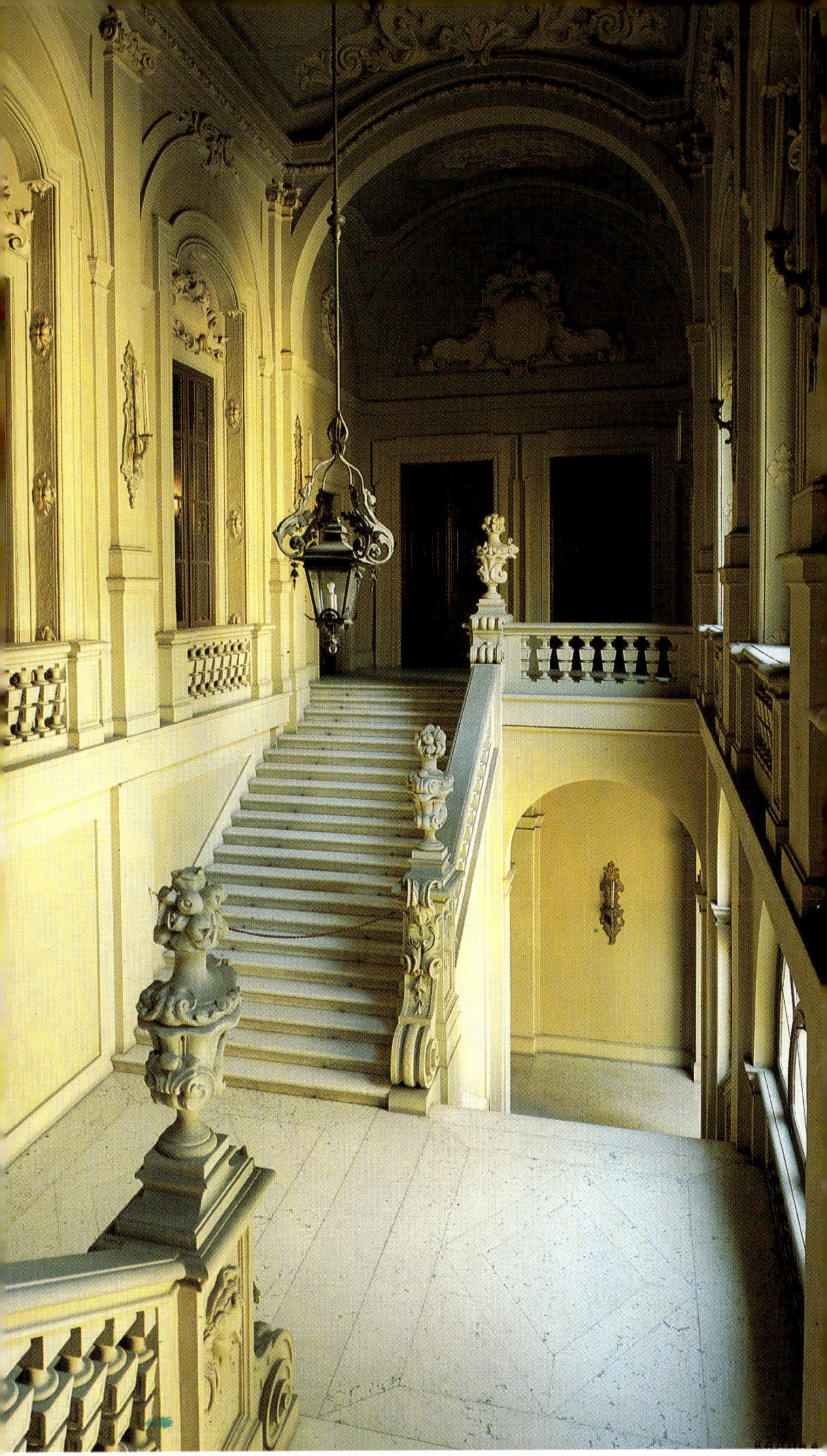

1

2

We turn back along via Tagliapietre and, in the square of the church of San Paolo, we see the start of via Val d'Aposa in front of us. A few yards down this street is a valuable XVI century oratory: it is that of the Holy Spirit and is attributed to Sperandio or to Vincenzo Onofri (others say instead to pupils of Nicolò dell'Arca). This was originally the church of Santa Maria dei Celestini and the temple kept this name until 1497 when it was conceded to the Brotherhood of the Holy Spirit. It has been restored many times through the centuries, and is a singular example of brickwork decoration.

Continuing along down via Val d'Aposa, we come to piazza Galileo, which is behind Palazzo d'Accursio. Here, walking past the Police Headquarters building and then turning left, we come to the Palazzo of the Government of Prefecture, formerly **Palazzo Caprara**. This actually consists of two buildings joined together and was built on the body of a pre-existing structure at the beginning of the 1600's, the work of Terribilia. The staircase, in two flights of a later date, is by Antonio Laghi. Inside are valuable works by Ludovico Carracci, Longhi, Marchesi, Gandolfi and others.

Next to Palazzo Caprara is via IV Novembre. On the right is another beautiful old palace, **Palazzo Marescalchi**, now the public administration offices for Architecture and the En-

1. The main steps (17th C) of the prefectorial Palazzo Caprara. 2. Piazza Roosevelt: to the right, Palazzo Caprara. 3. Via Ugo Bassi from the west.

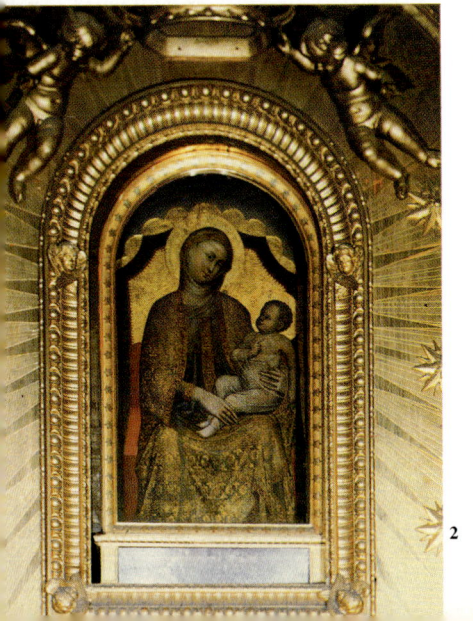

viranment. It goes back to the beginning of the 1600's and was erected on the foundations of a preexisting building. It is uncertain to whom it should be attributed: some say Tibaldi, others Mazenta. Inside is a valuable staircase and beautiful paintings and frescoes. Among the works of particular interest are those by Guido Reni, Tibaldi and Ludovico Carracci.

In the next house along, on April 25th 1874, as the memorial stone fixed to the façade commemorates, Guglielmo Marconi was born. In front of the Palazzo Marescalchi is the side of the splendid **church of San Salvatore**, with Roman characteristics, reconstructed on top of a preceding ancient temple around the beginning of the XVII century, to the design by Mazenta. The façade is somewhat similar to the church

3

4

of Santa Maria dei Monti in Rome. The interior, with a single nave, vaguely recalls a thermal room. Beautiful altars and splendid paintings decorate it. The tomb of Guercino in the centre of the church should be noted.

Leaving the church, we find ourselves almost directly opposite the old via Porta Nuova, which we walk along as far as the arch built in the XIII century in the wall of the Thousand, and passing this we return to piazza Malpighi. Turning right we thus come back into sight of the Two Towers, which stand out in the distance at the other end of the heart of the city. Turning our

1. St. Salvatore's Church (17th C). 2. Lippo (attr.): Madonna known as «of the Victory». 3. Carlo Bonomi: the Ascension of Christ. 4. Alessandro Tiarini: the Manger. 5. Tomb of Giovan Francesco Barbieri, known as «il Guercino» (the Squinter).

5

HEIC CINERES
FRATRVM PICTORVM
IOANNIS-FRANCISCI ET PAVLI-ANTONII BARBIERI
DOMO CENTO

CONCIVES
III·SAECVLO AB AVSPICATISSIMO NATALI·
IOANNIS FRANCISCI
VVLGO "GVERCINO„
P.

backs on them and passing next to the «Ospedaletto», already mentioned, we come out into **via San Felice**. This is one of the most characteristic Bolognese streets and preserves intact the flavour of the old city. There are many beautiful palazzos here too, often unexpected and concealed behind modest doorways and above porticos of narrow proportions. Of particular importance is the **palazzo Pederzani**, formerly Ariosti, built around 1730 on the remains of the preceding palazzo which the family (from which Ludovico Ariosto also descends) had on this site from two centuries earlier. The design is attributed to Dotti.

Further along this street is the **Palazzo Pallavicini** which has a beautiful staircase and valuable paintings inside.

From via San Felice, turning right along via dell'Abbadia, we come to the complex which now houses the military hospital and which was originally the convent and the **church of Saints Naborre and Felice**, built at the beginning of the XII century. It is said that the first Bolognese cathedral stood here, constructed by San Zama, bishop of the city, in 270 and therefore much earlier than the church of San Pietro and Paolo in the group of the «seven churches» of Santo Stefano. We then turn back towards the centre so as to begin the 4nd itinerary

1. The arch of Porta Nuova framing the bell tower of St. Francis'. 2. Via dell'Indipendenza from the south.

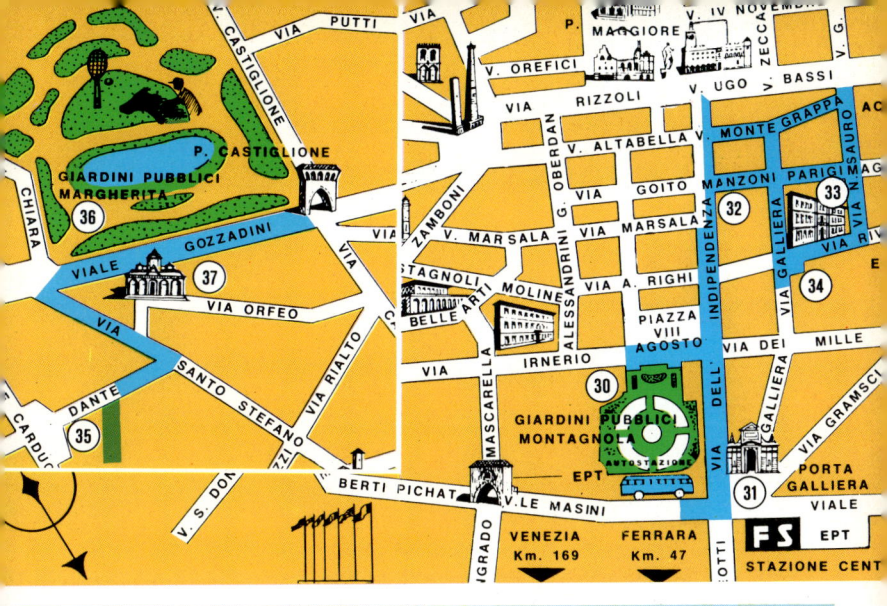

4th Itinerary

Summary:

30 Montagnola Public Gardens
31 Porta and Piazza Galliera
32 Church of Santa Maria di Galliera
33 Palazzo Montanari
34 Palazzo Tanari
35 House and Mausoleum of G. Carducci
36 Margherita Gardens
37 Church of Santa Maria del Baraccano

From the corner of via Ugo Bassi with via Indipendenza, we go along the later for a few yards and on our left we see the **palazzina Majani**, which is one of the best examples of liberty style in the city. It was designed by Augusto Sezanne. Looking out from under its portico, on the other side of the street we can see the **tower of the Scappi**, which often escapes the attention of the tourist, surrounded by all the beauty of piazza Nettuno and piazza Maggiore. It is 39 metres high and of the XIII century. It was absorbed into the palazzo built in the XVI century. We continue along via Indipendenza, (at the end of which one can admire the stairs of Pincio, the giardini della Montagnola, a park, and the remains of the ancient Castle of Galliera) passing on the right the church of San Pietro, already admired, and we come to via Manzoni, a side street on the left. Turning into this street, a little way ahead on the left, is **Palazzo Ghisilardi Fava**, the recent new seat of the Medieval and Renais-

2   1

3

4

sance Civic Museum, and amongst the most beautiful and antique of the city. Its foundantions enclose remains of the origins, perhaps, of the city: from the II century B.C. onwards through almost all the periods which have marked the evolution of the urban centre decisively. The innumerable restorations carried out on the building (some of which were mercilles and seriously depriving) have in fact brought to light traces of the ancient principal road, others of the circle of selenite (and the difference in level with the underlying road demonstrates the accumulation of earth piled against the walls), then more recent finds, from the Middle Ages to the birth of the actual

1. Porta Galliera (18th C). 2. Stair of the Pincio, built in 1893 by Tito Azzolini and Attilio Muggia. 3. Monument to the people in the Montagnola Gardens. 4. Fountain decorating the steps of the Pincio, by Diego Sarti. 4. Via Manzoni: courtyard of Palazzo Ghisilardi Fava (15th C).

5

palazzo now visible which was built towards the end of the 1400's. The façade with mullioned windows is beautiful; the pillars of the portico with their beautiful decorations are most artistic; above all, the courtyard with the double open gallery and the beautiful «brackets» is impressive.

In front of the palazzo Ghisilardi, is the **church of Santa Maria di Galliera**, known as «dei Filippini», with its beautiful Renaissance façade, all in sandstone. High up are two niches with figures of saints; at the centre is a beautiful rose-window. The rich stone «embroidery» which decorates the façade has unfortunately been damaged by time. The main door is vaguely reminiscent of that of the Certosa in Pavia. The interior is baroque and contains frescoes by Elisabetta Sirani and Annibale Carracci.

Continuing for a few yards and keeping the church on our right, we come out into via Galliera, antique and noble Bolognese street. Before walking along it, to admire the many beautiful palazzos found there, it is worth crossing the street and looking at the beginning of via Parigi, where there is an old oratory dedicated to the Madonna dell'Orazione and which houses the seat of the Association of War Invalidated

1. Church of the Madonna di Galliera: façade (1510). 2. Via Galliera: Palazzo Filippini. 3. Via Galliera, Palazzo Montanari, ex Aldrovandi. 4. St. Mary the Elder's Church (17th C) 5. Palazzo Felicini.

4

5

91

and Wounded. Inside are interesting paintings by Reni, by Domenichino and by students of Carracci. Almost opposite is the little street which finishes in the «Voltone dei Gessi», from the ancient palazzo by its side, now a hotel.

But let's return to via Galliera, the name of which is very old, even if deformed. In 1000 in fact, it was Galeria, seemingly in honour of the wife of Antonino Pio, Anna Galeria Faustina, to whom the locality bearing the name of Galliera in the hinterland of Bologna, is also dedicated. Why is this name commemorated? Perhaps because it constitutes the first recorded example of help for needy children, founded by Antonio Pio in the form of alimony: the «Faustinian alimentary girls», to honour the memory of his wife. If we wish to miss nothing of interest as we continue down via Galliera, we must cross the street several times passing from palazzo to palazzo. Right at the beginning, at no. 1, is the **palazzo Filippini**, from the name of the nearby church of the Filippini, at no. 3 is the **palazzo Dal Monte**, with a façade by Formigine and at no. 4 is **palazzo Zucchini**, rebuilt by Torreggiani. This artist, who has lavished Bologna with many gifts of talent and taste, is also responsible for, at no. 8, **palazzo Montanari**, formerly Aldrovandi, worth at least a partial visit. The palazzo should have been built under the direction of another architect. Angelini, who died before finishing the work. The façade is most impressive but the interior is beautiful too, particularly the staircase. Among the frescoes, which decorate the beautiful rooms, some of which house a section of the Communal Library, those of Bigari prevail. At the beginning of the 1800's the Aldrovandis had a famous ceramics factory here. After Palazzo Montanari, on our left is the old **church of Santa Maria Maggiore**, built in the XII century but modified several times. The last occasion was in the mid 1600's. The interior is impressive and houses valuable works of art of the XVIII century, the period to which certain parts of the façade date back.

Further ahead, on the corner with via Riva Reno, is **Palazzo Felicini**, built in 1497, one of the best preserved buildings of the period. The façade, in brickwork, has beautiful decorations. The courtyard and open gallery are elegant. Inside are many frescoes, paintings and marble busts by Algardi, Canuti, Alboresi and Colonna. Before crossing the street, to visit the other side of the square, it is worth looking at the palazzos which face onto the right-hand side, one of which, recently restored, ecloses one of the many towers of which the city is rich.

On the corner next to the church is the beautiful **Palazzo Tanari**, built at the beginning of the 1600's on a pre-existing building. The palazzo once contained several notable works of art, some of which have been lost or scattered with time. At present there is a statue by Provaglia and paintings by Martinelli and Valliani. In the past, the Tanaris were proud of their collection of paintings, among which were works by Guido Reni, Guercino, Ludovico and Annibale Carracci, now who knows where. The façade of the building is attributed to Gian Giacomo Monti.

Next to Palazzo Tanari is the XVI century **church of the Madonna della Pioggia**, which is the object of particular devotion. It was restored in the XVIII century. The internal decorations are valuable.

Turning into via Riva Reno, a few yards ahead on the left, is **Palazzo Scagliarini**, which now houses public

1. St. Giorgio in Poggiale: façade (16th-17th C). 2. St. Giorgio's and Sirio's Church façade (1780).

1

2

93

offices. By Taddini, it was built at the end of the XVIII century and displays harmonious and pleasing lines not only in the façade but also inside, particularly in the two courtyards. There is a beautiful staircase and valuable frescoes decorating several rooms, including some works by Gandolfi. Shortly after this palazzo, on the left we come to via Nazario Sauro, another old street with the various different denominations through the years. Here, a little further ahead, at no. 22, is the **church of San Giorgio**, recently restored after the damage caused by a bombardment in 1943, after which it was deconsecrated. It now houses works of art and documents collected by a bank of the city. During the restoration work, interesting Villanovian, Etruscan and other more recent archaeological remains found.

Further on again is **Palazzo Lambertini**, now a high school. Begun in 1570 and then enlarged with the demolition of several adjacent houses, it was more or less never finished. It was inhabited by the Lambertini family (from which descends the famous cardinal, later Pope Benedict XIV) for only a few years. Before becoming a high school, it housed a theatre for several years and then several public enterprises.

At the end of the street, on the left, is the ancient **church of Saints Gregorio and Siro**, whose bell-tower is formed by one of the many towers: this one belonged to **palazzo Ghisilieri**, formerly Caccialupi, before the XVI century. This church was built for the Venetian canons who were succeeded by other orders and it underwent several restorations, one of which indispensable and fundamental due to a terrible earthquake. The present-day façade dates back to the end of the XVIII century and is attributed to Venturoli. The interior houses several works by Formigine, saved from the disaster, and valuable paintings by Annibale Carracci, Procaccini and the Flemish Calvaert. The church also houses the tomb of Marcello Malpighi, famous biologist and considered the beginner of studies on embryology, which he taught in the Bolognese «studio».

Continuing along the last part of via Nazario Sauro, we find ourselves once again in via Ugo Bassi where, looking to the left, we can see yet again the Two Towers, eye-catching and dominating, under whose shadow the itineraries have begun and finished.

Those who do not want to miss anything in the city still have several possibilities, before dedicating time to the immediate environs of visiting some interesting aspects of it. For lovers of literature, leaving Bologna before having «taken leave» of the Carduccian mementos, would in fact be almost sacrilege. So here are a few «precious» indications: in via Broccaindosso, short

1. Tosti: Marble bust of the Poet. 2. House of Giosuè Carducci, once the church of Santa Maria del Piombo. 3. Leonardo Bistolfi: monument to Giosuè Carducci (1910-28).

and narrow side-street off strada Maggiore (not far from the Towers) is the poet's first house, that (to be precise) of the «pomegranate-tree». This tree, cut down to the roots by later inhabitants, did not die: the stump in the little garden threw out new branches which have withstood the passing of time. Not far from here, in the square dedicated to him, is the great monument by Bistolfi in liberty style, built very close to the last circle of walls. The monument depicts a thoughtful Carducci, surrounded by some of the «characters» from his works. Next to this is the house where he spent his last years, up to 1907, now a museum and library preserving precious curiosities: letters, autographs, his books, his pictures, his furniture: all donated to the city by queen Margherita who wanted to buy the house and give it to the Bolognese, for the future. For those that wish to admire another characteristic Bolognese attraction, they can visit the famous **Giardini Margherita** (Public Gardens) by following the ring road circling the perimeter of the walls. These gardens, with their vast surface area (55 hectares), have been the destination of the Bolognese of every class since the end of the 1800's. Inside the gardens, reconstructed «open to the sky», is one of the Etruscan tombs which emerged during excavations on the site.

In front of the gardens, is the **church of Baraccano**, close to the walls. This dates back to the 1400's and was rebuilt by Barelli. It has an interesting dome and a beautiful front. There are frescoes by Cossa inside the church.

1. The drawing room of Carducci's house. 2. Margherita Gardens: the pond. 3. Church of Santa Maria del Baraccano: the 1682 dome crowns the sixteenth-century temple.

2

3

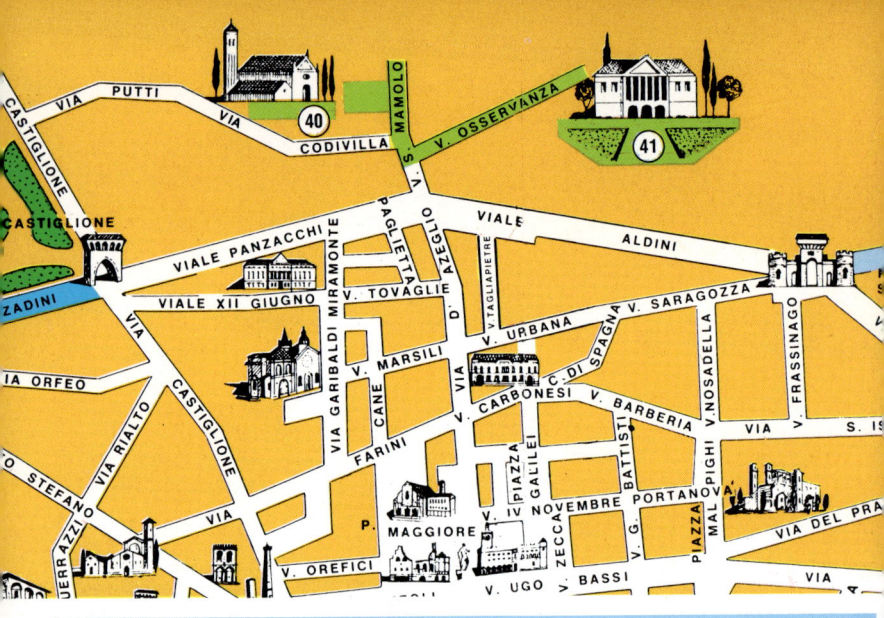

The environs

Summary:

38 Portico of St. Luke's and Meloncello
39 Sanctuary of the Madonna of Saint Luke
40 Church of San Michele in Bosco
41 Villa Aldini
42 Marzabotto - Etruscan City of Misa
43 Mausoleum of G. Marconi and Villa Griffone
44 Gallery of Modern Art

Having thus finished the visit to the city, we can think about improving our knowledge of Bologna by going to see some of the artistic beauties in the immediate outskirts and the environs. And the beginning could be a visit to the Colle della Guardia (Guardian Hill) where we find the temple of the

Madonna of San Luca, to which the Bolognese are particularly devoted. The church rises on the crown of one of the hills which are next to the city and is linked to it by a long portico of three and a half kilometres, which, beginning at porta Saragozza, reaches the top, giving amongst other things wide and very impressive views all around. The portico was of course built to give protection to the pilgrims, who have always gone up to the sanctuary, between the end of the 1600's and the beginning of the 1700's with the offers of the Bolognese. But the story of the church is much earlier than either the construction of the portico or of the church itself. It was in fact at the beginning of the XII century that a pilgrim by the name of Teocle, from the Orient, brought to Bologna, giving it to the Senate, an image of the Madonna with Child which for centuries had been kept in the church of Santa Sofia in Constantinople. The image, according to legend, was painted by the evangelist Saint Luke. Around it, a group of worshippers built a little chapel which became a well-known heremitage. With the passing of the centuries, the tiny building was gradually enlarged and the construction of the portico had already been begun, with 666 arches, one of which, the «Meloncello», is particularly elegant, when in the 1700's, the church which we can admire today was begun. The task was given to Dotti who constructed the imposing building in the form of a Greek cross, closed by an ellipse and surmounted by a great dome visible from all over the city. He is also responsible for the portico which, in the 366 arches from Meloncello to the church, has interesting «stages» in the «Mysteries». Every year, since the beginning of the 1400's, the image of the Madonna is brought down from the hill to reach the Cathedral of San Pietro where it remains for the eight days

1. Porta Saragozza, dating from the 14th C, enlarged in 1849. 2. The portico by Dotti which leads to the Church of the Madonna of St. Luke.

which lead up to Ascension Sunday, to receive homage from the faithful who then re-accompany it up the hill in a long procession.

Another very impressive church on

1. Basilica of the Madonna of Saint Luke, by Dotti (18th C). 2. The radiant interior of the Sanctuary. 3. A precious frontal view of the Madonna of Saint Luke. 4. Church of San Michele in Bosco (16th C).

4

the Bolognese hills is that of San Michele in Bosco. It was originally the church of the Olivetan monks, whose convent is now occupied by the famous Rizzoli orthopaedic institute. The construction of the church goes back as far as the IX century, even though it has been subjected to various modifications with the passing of the centuries. The biggest enlargement was made around the XV century, while the bell-tower

1. The large complex of San Michele in Bosco dominates the city. 2. The rich interior, decorated in the 16th-18th centuries. 3. Bagnacavallo: the Transfiguration.

102

was not finished until the XVIII century. Inside are splendid works by Guido Reni and Carracci, as well as others by notable artists of the period. The cloister is particularly impressive, now encompassed by «Rizzoli», octagonal in shape, and preserving the remains of many frescoes by Carracci. There are also two other traditional cloisters. The refectory and the library, with frescoes respectively by Vasari and Canuti, are very interesting.

Another hill worthy of note is that of San Vittore, on which rises the ancient convent of the monks dates back to the beginning of the XI century. From this period, it preserves the square apse, while the rest is of a later

2

1

period. Some remains, incorporated in the construction, lead us to believe however that even before the IX century, there was some religious construction on the site. The cloister is very beautiful and the interior is interesting, divided into two by a rood-screen. Many well known people lived in retreat and died in the convent. Their names are recorded in documents and memorial stones.

After San Vittore is another hill, that of the Observance, dominating the city and from which (in particular from via Marconi) we can admire the beautiful villa Aldini built there at the beginning of the 1800's for Napoleon. On the hill is the convent of the Minor Observant Friars and the church of San Paolo in Monte. Next to the villa is the oratory of the Madonna del Monte, with very old frescoes, the only remains of a bigger church demolished to build the villa Aldini.

On the same hill is the beautiful Monastery of Ronzano, inhabited ac-

1. Pietro Fiorini: the octagonal cloister (1602-1603). 2. Cenoby of San Vittore: the cloister (15th C). 3. Villa Aldini, neo-classical, surrounds the Romanesque rotonda of the Madonna del Monte. 4. Church of San Paolo in Monte dell'Osservanza (19th C).

105

cording to the friars of Loderingo degli Andalò, founder of the «Joyful Friars». On the site of the original monastery, there is now a church constructed by the Dominicans around the mid XV century, which contains valuable frescoes.

It is sufficient to go only a short way from the city to visit and admire other localities worthy of note.

Marzabotto, for example, the ancient Misa, is certainly worth a full visit. An Etruscan city of notable importance between the VI and the IV century B.C., it was discovered in relatively recent times by Gozzadini, noted Bolognese archaeologist, who su-

106

perintended the excavations. These were carried out by the wishes of Count Pompeo Aria, owner of a beautiful villa on the site, now restored after much damage during the war, and next to which is a museum housing numerous finds of great artistic and historic value. These excavations, begun in the 1800's, are still in progress and continue to reveal new aspects of the mysterious city. The necropolis is very interesting and can be visited together with the remains of the Acropolis. Marzabotto is unfortunately also known for the terrible massacre carried out by the German troops. A shrine, destination of pilgrims from all over the world, commemorates the innocent victims of this massacre.

Another interesting destination is Pontecchio, where we can see the villa Griffone in which Guglielmo Marconi carried out his first experiments in 1895, of telegraphy without wires. The villa, erected in the XVII century and acquired by the Marconis towards the end of the last century, now houses the institute of electronics of the faculty of Engineering of the University of Bologna. The villa is also the seat of the Marconi Foundation, preserving many mementos of the great scientist who rests in the mausoleum built at the foot of the hill on which the house stands.

Also at Pontecchio, is the interesting palazzo Rossi, now Bevilacqua Ariosti, built towards the end of the XV century. Several illustrious people stayed here: Giovanni Bentivoglio, the Pope Giulio II, Leone X, Paolo III and also Torquato Tasso. Apart from these two more famous localities however, there is practically no commune in the province which has not some masterpiece or other, often unknown or unheard of. We will mention a few without any order of merit, leaving the tourist the possibility of choice, according to the time available.

At Bentivoglio, for example, as well as a beautiful castle, the villa «Paleotta», and the museum of peasant civilization of S. Marino di Bentivoglio are

1. Church of the Most Holy Annunciation (15th C). 2. Marzabotto: eastern necropolis (detail). 3. The built-up area of the Etruscan city. 4. Tombs with emblems in the northern necropolis. 5. Pompeo Aria Archaeological Museum: the new wing.

worth a visit. At Budrio is villa Zambeccari, the Malvezzi villas, the Ranuzzi villas and palazzo Odorici. At Castenaso is villa Gozzadini, where the noted archaeologist lived, discoverer of the Villanovian settlements surrounding this villa and author of important research work on the subject. At Crespellano is the Garagnani Tower and the villas of Calcara. At San Martino in Soverzano di Minerbio is a castle. At Castagnolo di San Giovanni in Persiceto are the four towers of the same palazzo. At Vergato is the picturesque Mattei castle, built only in the last century but worth a visit for the jumble of styles of which it comprises. At Zola Predosa is the Albergati villa. And we should not forget the «fortresses»: the one at Bazzano, at Dozza and at Monteveglio. All an artistic heritage and in good condition due to the love and care of the owners.

1. Villa Griffone and mausoleum of Guglielmo Marconi. 2. Guglielmo Marconi. 3. Guglielmo Marconi on the Elettra, in the Genoese Port. 4. Marconi's yacht Elettra, named after the long experimentation conducted by the inventor in the post-war period. 5. Riola da Vergato: Church by Alvar Aalto, completed in 1978. 6. Riola di Vergato: the Mattei Citadel (19th C).

109

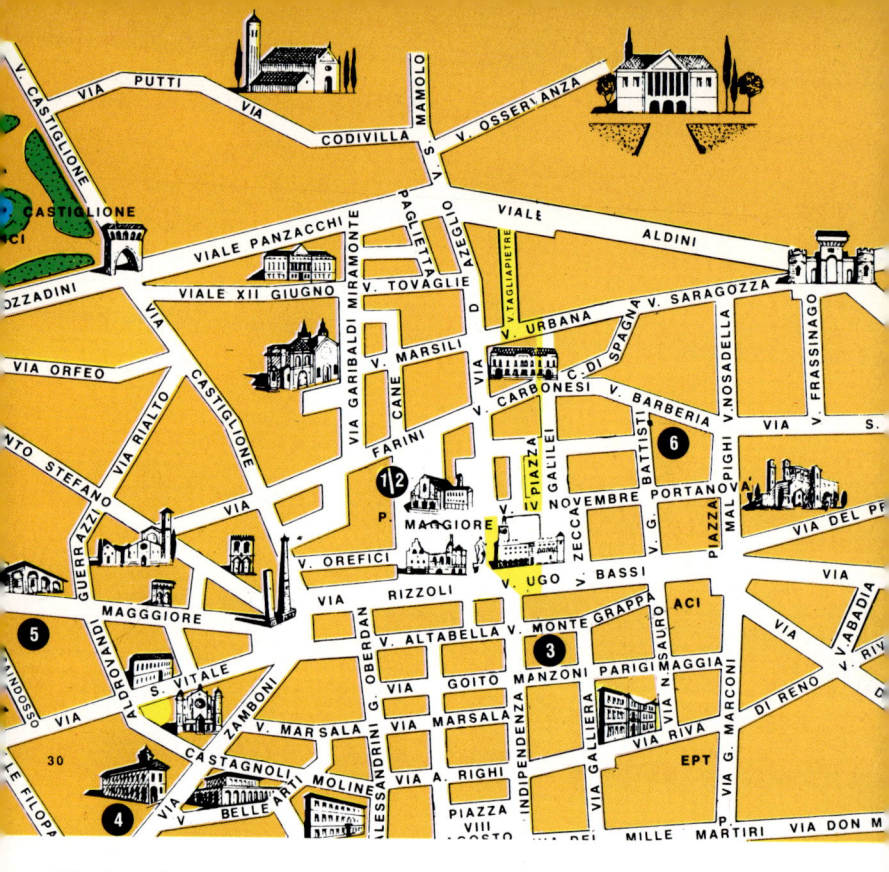

Civic Archaeological Museum

Beside St. Petronius's we find the Museo Civico Archeologico (the town's archeological museum) with its entrance at via dell'Archiginnasio n. 2. It was inaugurated on 25th September 1881 in the old palace of the Hospital of St. Mary of Death. The building, erected in the years 1336-39 and changed in 1565 by Antonio Morandi, also called Terribilia, through the addition of the arcade, was adapted to house a museum in 1875 following a design by Antonio Zannoni.

The museum was divided into different areas: the «Room of Antiquities» of the Institute of Sciences formed by the historical Aldrovandi, Cospi and Marsili collections, which later became the «Antiquarian Museum of the University»; the «Comunitativo Museum» formed by the Municipal art collection to which the Pelagi collection was added in 1860 and which became the «Civic Museum» in 1871. The new Archeological Civic Museum (which had a Medieval section until 1962, now moved to Palazzo Ghisilardi-Fava: see pag. 205), which in 1881 had already been endowed with the findings from the excavations carried out in 1871-81 in the necropolis of Villanova and Felsina, acquired later on the Capellini paleo-ethnological collection and the findings of the excavations carried out between 1881 and 1924.

In the hall and in the courtyard (previously the church and cloister of St. Mary of Death) we find the valuable exhibition of *gravestones*; in the hall there are also stones from the countryside and small urns from the ancient town, besides black and white mosaic floors from the town itself. Among all these Roman remains we would like to recall: the *Suarius Stela*, with a swine herder and 7 piglets; the *Stela of Q.*

Bologna's Museums

Legend:

① Civic Archaeological Museum
Via dell'Archiginnasio, 2

② Civic Museum of the First and Second Risorgimento
Via Musei, 8

③ Civic Museum of the Middle Ages and Renaissance
Via Manzoni, 4

④ Palazzo Poggi and University Museums
Via Zamboni, 33

⑤ Civic Museum of Industrial Art, and Davia Bargellini Gallery
Strada Maggiore, 44

⑥ Didactic History Tapestry Museum
Via Barberia 13. After November 1989, Via Casaglia, 1

Manilius Cordo, a pseudo-aedicule; the *Stela of the Togaed Man*, from Maccaretolo; the *limestone Sphynx*, from Borgo Panigale; the beautiful marble *loricaed bust*, thought to be a statue of Nero (1st cent. A.D., originally from Piazza dei Celestini).

Also, we can admire two big *cylindrical Etruscan altars*, finely relief-decorated monoliths from the 7th century B.C. which were found in 1985 in an ancient sacred ground in today's via Fondazza.

In the courtyard, besides the numerous Classical, Greek, Roman and Christian inscriptions, we can see a beautiful *entablature* in Luni marble from Rodriguez palace; the series of *milestones* from *via Aemilia* are quite impressive: the highest one, 3.30 m, comes from areas around the Reno river and was dedicated to Augustus, the restorer of life.

The main collections of the Museum are on the first floor: Egyptian, Greek and Roman, Italian-Etruscan, Etrus— can, archeological finds in the area of Bologna, the burial grounds of Villanova and the excavations of Antonio Zannoni, remains from Pre-Roman Bologna, from the Paleolithic and Iron Ages, and Celtic finds. Room I, Prehistory (manufacts found in the area of Bologna): to be noted *41 bronze axes* from Rocca di Badolo (show-case IV), *sandstone cast die for a sickle and two arrow-heads* from Priosta di Imola (show-case VII), *ossuaries* and *ashes urns* from the necropolis of Pragatto

Glimpse of the courtyard.

1. Loricata, Roman marble statue (1st C). 2. The robed figure in Maccaretolo, Roman statue, and the «suariu» grave stele. 3. Grave stele of the Cornelii (1st C b.C.). 4. Egyptian relics: group of statues of the married couple Amenhotep and Merit (18th-19th dynasty).

(show-case IX), *finds from the «hut of the gold ornaments»* from Borgo Panigale, and *three zoomorphic figurines* (show-case XI). Room II, Prehistoric parallelisms.

Egyptian Antiquities (rooms III, IV, V). This collection, bought by Pelagio Palagi in 1831 from Giuseppe Nizzoli, the chancellor of the Austrian Consulate in Cairo, and donated by Palagi to the town in 1860, is the third in order of importance after Turin and Florence. In it we can admire all the classes of monuments, from amulets to scarabs (more than 2,000 pieces), to *shuebte* or burial statuettes (over 400 pieces), to mummies, painted sarcophagi, papyruses, funerary urns, to large and small stone and bronze statues, to relief works and funerary stelae.

The so-called «New Kingdom» is particularly well documented. Room III: in the centre, *Portrait of King Amenhophis IV*, in black granite (18th dynasty); limestone *funerary stela* with relief works for the King Horemheb at Saqqara (19th dynasty, 1354-1346 B.C.); *wall panels from the tomb of Horemheb*, the general of Amenhophis IV (18th dynasty). Room IV: a black granite *statuette of a seated dignitary*, wearing a wig; it is the oldest piece in the Egyptian collection, and it dates back to the 4th dynasty (24th century B.C.); *statues of husband and wife* (the priest Amenhotep and his wife Merit, in limestone, 18th-19th dynasty); a rich collection of *shuebte*, of which we should mention the pieces from the tomb of the Pharaoh Sethi I (1318-1304 B.C.); the *Book of the dead* of the 19th dynasty; the marvellous *wooden statue of the naked girl*; the limestone *statue of the king's scribe Amenmes* offering the votive images of Osiris, Isis and Ho-

1. Relief on the wall of the tomb of Horemheb. 2. Shuebte of King Seti I, in blue majolica.

rus (19th dynasty); painted sarcophagi, painted boxes with the shape of mummies, mummies (a peculiar one is the *cat's mummy*), Room V: a granite *group of two statues of gods*, the vulture and the hawk (26th dynasty); the beautiful *Relief work of the King Nectanebo I* in black granite (30th dynasty); burial boxes, funerary stelae, votive relief works, amulets, scarabs, etc.

Greek Antiquities. Room VI: the magnificent *Palagi's Head*, or *Lemnian Athena*, Pentelic marble, a copy made at the time of Augustus from a 5th century B.C. bronze attributed to Phidias. In the show-cases: amphorae, one of which is the *decorated amphora with handles shaped as ribbons*, an Attic ceramic work with black figures by the Greek Nikosthenes from the 6th cent. B.C.; oinochoe, craters, lekytoi or balm urns, skyphos, pelike, hydrias, kantaros. Among the kylikes (table vases) we would like to mention the world-famous *Codro's Cup*, from Vulci in Phidian style from the 5th century B.C.; there are also many clay statuettes, a precious group of *Tanagra* statuines, small bronzes, ceramics, votive reliefs, etc. **Roman Antiquities**. Room IX: *cylindrical altar* in marble from Boncellino (Bagnacavallo) with pairs of cornucopias; *bronze trypod* from the last years of the Roman Empire; a marble *head of putto*; a nice

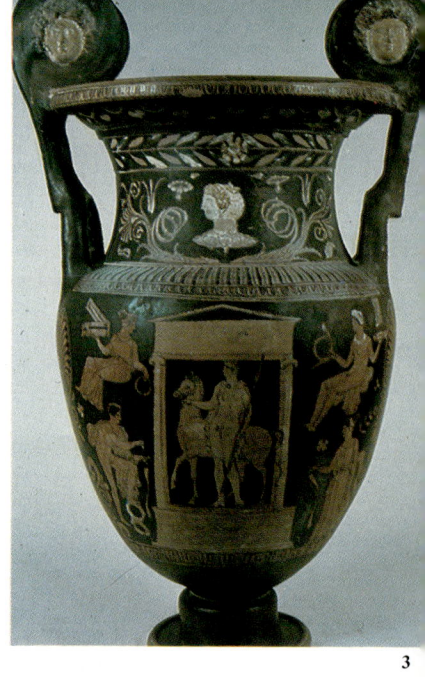

114

porphyry basin; and also: small bronzes, ivories, pieces of roof tiles, amphorae, terracotta lamps, surgical instruments, scales, weapons, statues, capitals, metopes, terms, etc. Room VII: a *statue probably representing an Emperor*; a superb *bust from a Ionian statue*, perhaps a nude of an athlete, in marble from the 2nd century A.D.; a *bust of Aphrodite bathing*, a copy from the work of Doidalses of Bitinia (3rd century B.C.).

Italic-Etruscan Antiquities. Room VIII: two marvellous *alabaster urns* from Volterra (2nd cent. B.C.); Etruscan canopic vases, male and female terracotta heads, clay votive offerings, buccheri, painted Etruscan ceramics, tombs' furnishings; remains of the *choroplastic frieze of Civitalba* near Sassoferrato in the Marche (2nd century B.C.), with terracotta composi-tions representing Dionysus and Ariadne and the flight of the Gauls from Delphi; *urns from Chiusi* in relief terracotta.

Villanovan Antiquities, from the end of the 10th century to the first half of the 6th century B.C.. The Villanovan culture, on which the Etruscan colonization had good hold, takes its name from the excavation carried out at Villanova of Castenaso by Giovanni Gozzadini, after the discovery of the necropolis with 193 tombs in 1853. At that time the precious finds threw some light on the past of Bologna by allowing hypotheses on the Pre-Roman cultures around the town to be formulated. These hypotheses were later confirmed by the excavations carried out by Antonio Zannoni (necropolis of Certosa with 421 tombs from Felsina in 1869) and by the ones made by Gozzadini himself at Marzabotto, besides those by Prizio and others. The findings fill the Rooms Xa, X and Xb, and they are so numerous that it is impossible to describe them here in this guidebook. We would like to mention the sandstone *Gozzadini Head* with a cu-

Statue of Uahibra, in black granite (26th dynasty). 2. Head of Atena Lemni, Greek copy from Fidia. 3. Apulian crater in Volute (4th C b.C.). 4. Attic kylix with red terracotta figures. Palagi Collection (450-425 b.C.).

115

1

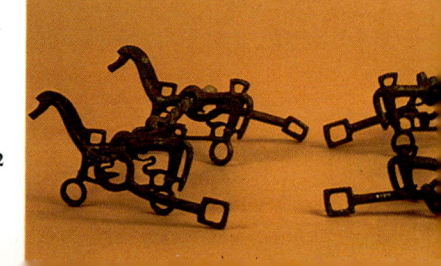

2

3

4

bic structure (6th century B.C.); the famous *Benacci askos* in the shape of an animal, whose handles are two stylized horses, a terracotta work from the 7th century B.C.; the series of objects (14,841) found in 1877 by Zannoni in the «closet of St. Francis».

The Etruscan Civilization: this is Europe's most important Etruscan collection and it is exhibited in the large rooms X and XI. In this case as well, it is impossible for us to give a detailed description of all the items. Room X: the *Arnoaldi Situla*, in the shape of a truncate cone (5th century B.C.); *head of kouros* (young man) in white marble from around 500 B.C., in deposit from the Marzabotto Museum; *small bronzes* from the votive drawer (ca. 480 B.C.) of the mountain shrine of Monte Acuto Ragazza; *small bronzes*, ca. 430

1. Askòs Benacci, from Villanova (8th C b.C.).
2. Biconical ossuary with bowl, Villanova (8th-9th C b.C.). 3. Etruscan tomb of the Certosa cemetary: attic crater with red figures and other objects which make up the set. 4. Bronzed horse jaws from the Villanova necropolis Benacci-Caprara . 5. Bronze Etruscan situla, from Certosa (5th C b.C.). 6. Detail of the situla showing the procession of the lance-armed warriors. 7. Etruscan horseshoe stele, from Certosa (4th C. b.C.).

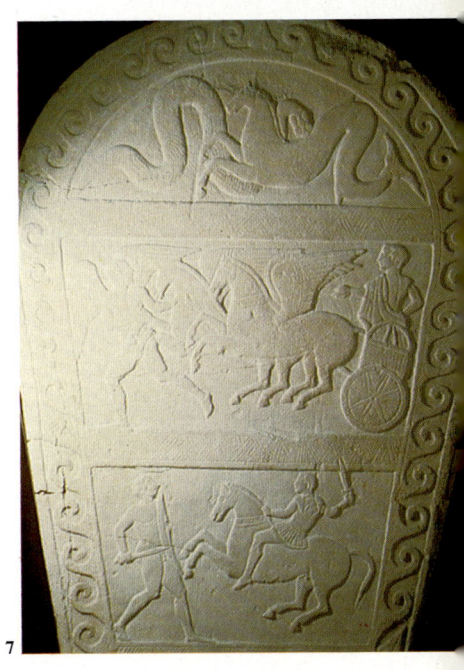

B.C., from Monte Capra. Among the many beautiful gravestone stelae, let us mention the *Big stela of the Giardini Margherita*, 5th century B.C., built for the deceased Vele Caicne. The famous *Situla of Certosa*, in the shape of a

117

truncate cone, in bronze sheet, with four bands of relief figures (6th-5th centuries B.C.); the furnishings of the *Big Tomb* from the Giardini Margherita, the richest of the ones found in the Felsina's necropoles, with a *wood chest* measuring 3.5 m. x 2.5 m.; the furnishings of the *Tomb of the stool* from the Giardini Margherita, 5th century B.C., in which a folding *ivory stool* is carved, the only example of such an object made from that material.

Roman and Gallic Civilizations. Room XII: the main aspects of the Gallic culture which grafted on to the Etruscan civilization in the 6th century B.C. and in the 2nd century gave place to the Roman one are illustrated here together with specific characteristics of the Roman civilization typical of the Bologna's area. From the Gallic burial grounds: *two helmets* in bronze from the 3rd century B.C.; *gold diadem* with lanceolate leaves on oval gold sheets; a *bronze vase* in the shape of situla with modelled handle; a *oinochoe* with a three-lobed mouth and the handle shaped as a naked dancing boy; a *cap helmet* with gold embossed discs on the ear flaps; *iron sword* with bone hilt, 3rd century B.C.; candlesticks, mirrors,

1. A worshiper: Etruscan bronze from Monte Acuto Ragazza (5th C b.C.). 2. Gallic tiara made of gold (4th-3rd C b.C.). 4. Bronze wine jug (4th-3rd C b.C.).

fibulae (bucles), armillae (armlets), shears, clay objects, andirons, bronzes, painted and unpainted ceramics. Roman antiquities: *Figure of a nymph lying on one side*, the decoration of a fountain from the 3rd century B.C.; *Cyma of a stela* with four portraits of men; *Relief* with scenes of gladiators from a sepulchral monuments; three *silver cups*, Roman-Hellenistic art; *clay bust* of running Eros. We can mention various objects in a show-case, such us a small bronze of *Barbarian horseman* from Claterna; a small bronze of *Diana* from Monteveglio; a terracotta *Eros* (1st century A.D.).

The Civic Archeological Museum is open from 9 a.m. to 2 p.m. from Tuesday through Saturday; on Sunday from 9 a.m. to 12.30 p.m. The museum is closed on Monday and on holidays falling during the week.

Civic Museum of the First and Second Risorgimento

A large section of the ground floor, where the infirmary of the Hospital of St. Mary of Death once was (the vast halls facing the Museum, where temporary exhibitions are held, were also part of the infirmary) is now occupied by the Museo Civico del I e del II Risorgimento. The Museum was arranged in its definite layout in 1975 to exhibit a vast selection of items relating to the Risorgimento and the Resistance: paintings, uniforms, flags, weapons, printed matters, autographs, busts and other historical mementoes, which testify of the active participation of the town and its people in the struggle for indipendence in the 19th century and the battle for freedom against the yoke of the Fascist and Nazi occupation.

Paintings: *Portrait of Pope Pius IX* by Francesco Zauli Sajani; *The Austrians Driven out of Town through Gal-*

119

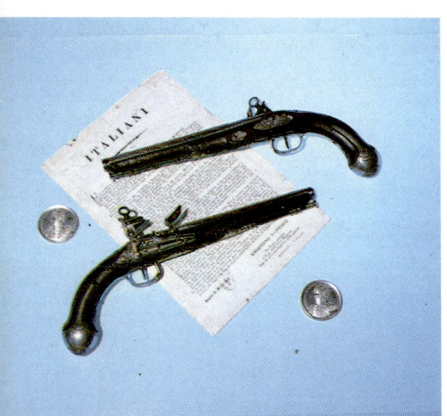

liera Gate by Antonio Muzzi; *Ugo Bassi at the Pia Column* by G. Belvederi; *Ugo Bassi in the Comacchio Gaol* by Carlo Ademollo; *Dancing around the Freedom Tree* by Belvederi; *The Battle of Lame Gate* by Lorenzo Ceregato; *Death of the Partisan* by Emilio Contini.

The museum is open from 9 a.m. to 2 p.m. from Tuesday to Saturday. On Sunday from 9 a.m. to 12.30 p.m.. The museum is closed on Monday and holidays falling during the week.

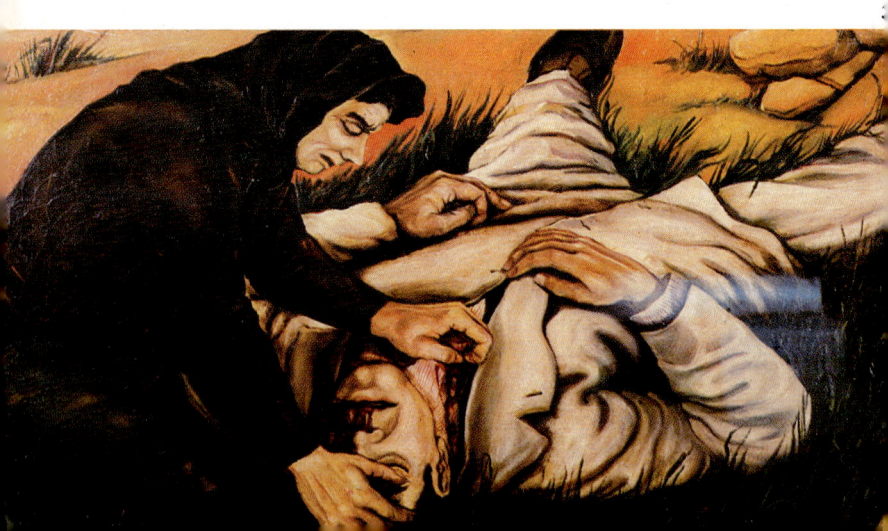

Civic Museum of the Middle Ages and Renaissance

The Museo Civico Medievale e del Rinascimento (Civic Museum of Medieval and Renaissance Art) is located in **Palazzo Ghisilardi-Fava**, via Manzoni 4.

Opened in spring of 1985, this museum is located in a nice palace built between 1483 and 1491 according to a plan by master Zilio (Egidio) Montanari for the grand notary and chancellor of the Sixteen, Bartolomeo Ghisilardi. Bought by the Counts Fava in 1810 and later passed to the Municipality, this building has been brought, through extensive restoration works carried out for over a decade with the most sophisticated and scientific criteria, to its pristine condition, by eliminating all the foreign elements that had been added in various times. The original structure has been strengthened and brought to light (for which, together with Palazzo Sanuti Bevilacqua, see pag. 168, it is considered the most complete and magnificent example of civilian architecture of 15th-century Bologna) and, through the restoration, the finding and identification of important older buildings have been made possible. Among these older structures, let us recall: the *Conoscenti tower* from the 13th century, and the remains (selenite ashlar wall section, coupled arches formed by blocks in the same material) of the *Palatium*, seat of the political and military powers in the town, located on the north-western side of the *selenite town's walls* from the mid-7th century (large sections of which have now been shown) and demolished in 1115. The collections, which from 1881 to 1962 formed the Medieval section of the Museo Civico (today's formed only by the extremely important archeological section and therefore called Museo Civico Archeologico, see pag. 88) in the former Hospital of Death, were originally part of the Museum of Ferdinando Cospi (1605-1686), of the artworks arranged in Palazzo Poggi by Marsigli in 1709-12, and also included the floor gravestones and tombs belonging to suppressed churches, assembled together from 1866 onwards by Luigi Frati. Other older pieces, collected by Aldrovandi, or other ones from the 19th century by Palagi have come to this museum. Its aim is to illustrate the development of Medieval and early Renaissance art in Bologna, with many examples of Baroque and Mannerist art as well, in a logical and exhaustive approach including the links between the town and the Studium and the artistic circles and workshops in Italy and abroad. The so-called «minor arts» are particularly well attended to (ivory pieces, ceramics, glass objects, medals

1. A. Muzzi: the banishment of the Austrians from Porta Galliera. 2. Pistols and medals of Murat, in a copy of the «Rimini Proclamation» (1818). 3. E. Contini: the death of the resistance fighter. 4. Via Manzoni: courtyard of the Palazzo Ghisilardi Fava.

and coins, musical instruments, textiles, weapons, etc.) in a thorough exhibit ranging from the period in which Bologna was a Free-town to the one in which it was ruled by the Bentivoglio family, together with pieces from the «historical» collections. The future enlargement of the museum, by opening the connecting Palazzo Fava (16th century) will allow the exhibit of ceramics and musical instruments in five rooms frescoed by the Carracci painters in 1584.

All the items in the museum are accompanied by clear captions and explanations. The rational layout of the museum within a historical palace makes a visit to Palazzo Ghisilardi really worthwhile, and probably one of the most evocative in Italy.

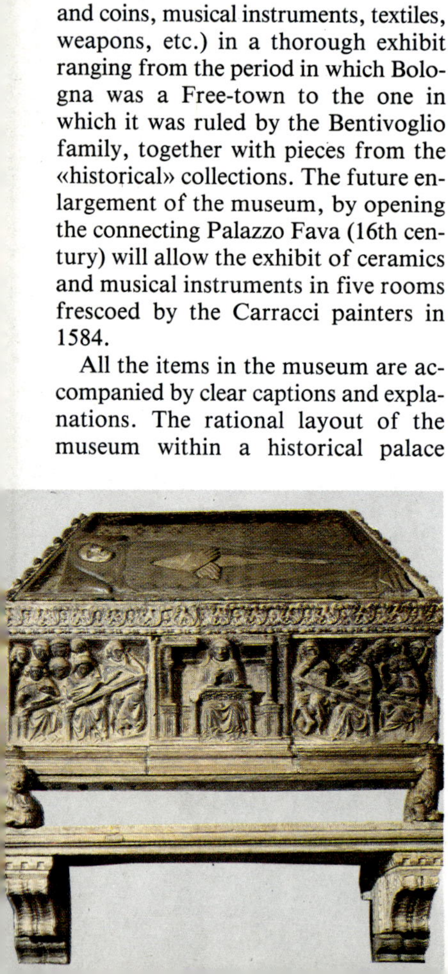

Ground floor. Room 4, called of the Monuments to the Studium's teachers: *Ark of Giovanni d'Andrea*, 1348, a marble work by Jacopo Lanfranchi from Venice; *Fragments of the ark of Giovanni da Legnano*, 1383, by Pier Paolo Dalle Masegne; *Fragments of the ark of Carlo, Roberto and Riccardo da Saliceto*, 1403, by an unknown stone carver; *Ark of Bartolomeo da Saliceto*, 1411, a marble work by Andrea da Fiesole. In all the monuments for the University teachers found in this museum, and in all the floor gravestones, we should notice the extraordinary naturalism and extreme liveliness of expression of the carved images. Room 5: jewellery, a *lombard cross* in gold leaf from the 8th century. Room 6, monuments of various origins: a stone *cross* on a column, and a *cross with the «agnus dei»*, also in stone, both from the 12th-13th centuries; *bronze handwashing vessel* from Lower Saxony, 13th century; *Prayer in the Garden*, a carved ivory work of art from Northern Italy, 12th century. Room 7: *base of a stoup* with four male figures by a sculptor from the Po valley area, 13th century; *St. Ursula*, an embossed cop-

1. Civic Medieval Museum: road crosses from the 12th-13th centuries. 2. The Arch of Giovanni di Andrea, by Jacopo Lanfrani. 3. Pier Paolo dalle Masegne: fragment of the Arch of Giovanni di Legnano, 1383. 4. Manno da Siena: Boniface VIII (1301). 5. Giovanni di Balduccio: St. Peter the Martyr.

Giovanni di Balduccio; the *Peace stone* by the «master of Corrado Fogolini» from 1322, carved in celebration of the settling of a controversy risen between the students and the town. Room 10: *Tomb of Pietro Cerniti*, 1338, a stone work by Roso da Parma; the famous *Floor gravestone of Domenico Garganelli*, made around 1478 by Francesco del Cossa in limestone, variegated marble and bronze; the *Tomb of Bonifacio Galluzzi*, 1346, a variegated Istrian stone work by Bettino da Bologna; *Statue of the Virgin with Child*, called St. Mary of Bethlehem, a marble work from the 13th century. Room 11: *Tomb of Lorenzo Pini*, 1397, by per piece from the 14th century; a *statue of Pope Bonifatius VIII*, an exceptional piece in embossed copper over a wooden core by Manno Bandini from Siena, 1301; *Crucifixion*, a European painted glass, 13th century; anthropomorphic bronze *candlestick* from Lower Saxony, 13th century; an extraordinary *cope of St. Dominic* (from St. Dominic's church), an English piece in linen and silk from the beginning of the 14th century, embroidered with 19 tales of the life of Christ and Mary and figures of angels and saints.

Basement. Room 8: *Gravestone of Filippino Desideri* by Arriguzzo Trevisano, 1315. Room 9: *Statue of St. Peter Martyr*, a marble work by

Paolo di Bonaiuti. Room 12: powerful marble triptych (*Virgin with Child*, *Saints Peter and George*, *Angels* and a *Saint* in the only remining cusp) by Jacopo della Quercia and his workshop from the beginning of the 15th century; *Nativity scene*, a marble high-relief by Andrea da Fiesole. Room 13: *Floor gravestone of Bernardino Zambeccari*, a stone work by Andrea da Fiesole, 1424; *Tomb slab of Pietro Canonici*, a variegated stone work by Vincenzo Onofri, 1502; *Tomb of Matteo Gandoni*, 1330, from the workshop of Agostino di Giovanni and Angelo di Ventura.

First floor. Room 15: bronze statues and figurines from the Renaissance to the Baroque period: *Model of the Neptune's statue* for the Fountain on the square, by Giambologna, 1564; the *Archangel Michael* by Alessandro Algardi; a *bust of Gregory XIII Boncompagni* by Alessandro Menganti, 1572; *bust of Gregory XV Ludovisi*, attributed to Gian Lorenzo Bernini, ca. 1621; among the bronze statuettes, *Marsyas* and the *Burial of Christ* by Andrea Briosco, known as Riccio; small *casket* with reliefs attributed to Severo di Ravenna (all works from the 16th century) and also sculptures by Vittoria, Aspetti, Giambologna, Campagna. Room 16: part of the collection of musical instruments from Europe and other parts of the world, especially from the 16th and 17th centuries, is temporarily shown here as the permanent exhibition rooms, frescoed by the Carracci painters, in Palazzo Fava are being restored. The collection comprises many valuable pieces, such as: a *clavichord* by Vito de Transuntini, 1606; a *bass lute* by M. Stegher, 16th century; a *lute* by Magnus Tieffenbrucker junior, 1612; a *harpsychord* by Orazio Albana, 1628; a *larg mandolin* by Matteo Sellas, 1630; a *pochette* shaped as a dolphin by B. Bressano; a *psaltery* by Francesco Cessori, 18th

1. «Stone of Peace», 1322 (detail). 2. Francesco del Cossa: the ground slab of Domico Garganelli (circa 1478). 3. Bettino da Bologna: Sepulchre of Bonifacio Galluzzi (1346). 4. Madonna of Bethlehem (13th C).

century. Rooms 17 and 18: weapons, blades and fire-arms, mostly from the Crespi and Marsigli collections, including a *Blessed rapier* in steel and silver made in Rome in the 15th century for Ludovico Bentivoglio; a *plaque with St. George*, a painting by a follower of Francia, on a parchment stretched over a wood frame; a *composite armour for open battle* from Northern Italy, ca. 1570; a 15th- century *horn* from the times of the Bentivoglio, a work from Emilia; a *cinquedea dagger*, etched with the Bentivoglio coat of arms, ca. 1500; a decorated and embossed *brocchiere* from the Milan school at the end of the 16th century; and also a stucco, *Veronica* by Francesco di Simone Ferrucci from Fiesole (15th century); a *glass tondo with a male head*, 15th century, attributed to Ercole Roberti; *stained-glass with Christ in Pietà* by an artist from Bologna, 15th century. Rooms 19 and 20 displaying Turkish weapons and others: a *pair of tschinken* (light archebus) with the Marsigli coat of arms from the 17th century (Silesia); *quivers* for arrows and bow, 17th century. Room 21, ivory and bone objects: a *box with the myth of Pyramos and Thysbe*, Embriachi workshop, 15th century; *triptych with the Virgin and Child* and *scenes of the life of Christ*, a 14th-century French production; an African-Portuguese ivory *salt-box*, 15-16th centuries; *basin* with the stories of David, in ivory, deer antlers and metal by J. M. Maucher from Germany (17th century). Room 22, glass: a *cou-

Ferrara, Imola, Bologna, Urbino, Pesaro, Castel Durante — later Urbania —, Lodi, Venezia, Albisola, Savona, Castelli, Cafaggiolo, Montelupo, Gubbio, etc.). Among the pieces from abroad, let us recall the ones from Spain of Arabic inspiration (Manises) and Germany (Siegburg, Köln, Frechen, Kreussen, Westerwald, etc.). We would like to mention: the *ink-well with 4 Patron Saints of Bologna*, a majolica from Faenza, 15th century; a *jug with a lady's bust* pierced by a dagger and the inscription «Love», a majolica from Faenza, 1499; a *cup with Clement VII crowning Charles V*, a majolica of Casa Pirota, Faenza, ca. 1530; a *tagliere (plate) with the grief over a warrior-woman*, a majolica by Baldassarre Manara, Faenza ca. 1534; a *cup with Jesus in the house of Simon*, by Leonardo Solombrino, a majolica from Forlì from 1564; *albarello vase* with bearded old man, a majolica from Venice, ca. 1570; *tagliere with the dream of Astiage*, a majolica by Francesco Xanto Avelli, Urbino 1536; *tagliere with Adonis and Mhyrra*, a majolica by Niccolò Pellipario from

ple *of bottles from Murano* from the 15th century with the Bentivoglio and Sforza coats of arms; a *blue goblet*, decorated and gilded from Murano, 15th century; a *goblet* with small handles from Murano, 16th century; interlaced *display plate* from Murano, 16th century; small *cup* in blown-glass and filigree from Murano, 18th century; a magnificent *perfume vial* made in Mesopothamia and Assyria in the 13th century.

The really valuable *collection of ceramics*, still to be arranged in the rooms of Palazzo Fava, comprises about 300 pieces which illustrate the amazing development of this production from the 13th to the 19th centuries; it also exhibits pieces from many kilns and workshops, some more famous than others but all very interesting (Faenza,

1. Giambologna: sketch of Neptune. 2. Niccolò Pellipario: dish illustrated with Adone and Mirra, circa 1575. 3. Plate of Saint George, from the Francia group.

126

Urbino, 1525; *plate decorated with the Presentation of the Virgin*, 1532, majolica by Niccolò Pellipario polished in Gubbio by Giorgio Andreoli; a *trilobate basin with the triumph of Galathea* by Fontana from Urbino, ca. 1575; *Bacchus and Sylenus*, round earthenware from the Aldrovandi kilns in Bologna, end of the 18th century. The section on the grès from the Reno valley is also quite interesting (Colle Ameno of the Ghisilieri).

The *collection of codes and miniatures* comprises about 140 codes with matriculae, statutes and chorals, especially from the 13th to the 15th centuries in Bologna: the *matricula of the Drapers* is quite famous, a 1411 miniature from Bologna, reproducing the lively activity of the «middle Market». The collection of *medals* is really important; with its thousands of medals and coins, it illustrates the production of the Bologna's Mint along the centuries and it comprises really invaluable artistic and historical pieces. Among the Bentivoglio coins, let us recall the famous *testone* by the painter and goldsmith Francia and, among the medals, exceptional pieces by Pisanello and Sperandio from the 15th century.

In February 1988 a new section (two rooms) was opened; in it, the atmosphere of the Baroque *rooms of wonders* has been created in order to stress the continuous interest for near and far civilizations, which has always characterized the cultural life of Bologna and its people, in the past as in the present. This exhibit comprises about 350 pieces from some of the most prestigious collections of Bologna, such as the Cospi and Palagi ones, whose items come from Italy and Europe, Latin America, Africa and Asia.

In the nearby Neo-Gothic building, called *Castellaccio* and built as a horseshed after 1810, we can see the *Medieval and Renaissance lapidary* with important pieces, such as the *slab of the bambagina paper*, the *Renaissance Hebrew stelae* and the controversial *inscription of Aelia Lelia Crispis* (this one a historical-literary curiosity).

Nearby we can admire architectural and decorative fragments dating back to the Romanesque period and the following ones, such as the *Gothic mullioned window* from St. James's or the big sandstone *Dalla Rovere coats of arms*.

Visits on weekdays from 9 a.m. to 2 p.m.; on Sundays from 9 a.m. to 12,30 p.m.. The Museum is closed on Tuesday and on holidays falling within the week. Telephone n. 228912.

Palazzo Poggi and University Museums

Palazzo Poggi, in via Zamboni 3, has been the central seat of the University and the Rector's office since 1803. It was built between 1549 and 1560 following a design by Pellegrino Tibaldi and/or Bartolomeo Triachini as the noble and sumptuous home for Alessandro Poggi and his brother, the Cardinal Giovanni. It is magnificently decorated inside (the frescoes portraying mithological and Biblical scenes are by Pellegrino Tibaldi, and the ones with landscapes and scenes from everyday life are by Nicolò dell'Abate). The *Tower of the Specola* rises above it: it was started in 1712-13 according to a plan by Giuseppe Antonio Torri and was completed by Carlo Francesco Dotti in 1723-25. At that time, Palazzo Poggi became the seat of the *Institute of Sciences*, according to the will of Luigi Ferdinando Marsigli, who had founded it in 1711 and inaugurated in 1714. At the opening of the arcade from Largo Trombetti we can see the symbol of Bologna's old student fraternity, the marble *fittone delle Spaderie*, a kerbstone placed in 1870 in the Spaderie street, no longer existing now. The «fittone» was placed where it now stands in 1912. It was restored in 1984.

The building houses, besides many University's offices and institutes, rooms and exhibits of exceptional interest especially for their scientific and cultural value. The itineraries established for a thorough visit of these important exhibits start at the ground floor, from the *Carducci Lecture Hall*, in which the great Poet had held his classes on Italian literature from 1860 onward, for 43 years. Here we can see the old desks occupied by many famous students, here the flamboyant author of the «Odi Barbare» is portrayed in a bronze bust made in Rome by Bastianelli. The room facing this lecture hall is called the *Hercules Room* because the restored sandstone statue of Hercules, sculpted by Angelo Piò around 1730 and placed up to a few years back in the courtyard to which it gave its name, was later on placed here (a copy was put on the old pedestal). The tour of the museums of Palazzo

1. Hercules, by Angelo Piò, at the Palazzo Poggi. 2. Giosuè Carducci's Aula. 3. Rectorial signs of the studio (16th C). 4. Le Bien Aimé. 5. Le Royal Louis, 1630 model.

3

Poggi offers the visitor the invaluable scientific and cultural contribution given by the Institutes of Sciences of Bologna (which had been active in this location for the whole 18th century) through its laboratories and historical collections out of which the majority of the Bologna University's museum, including the scientific ones, have sprung up. They form one of the most important institutions of this kind in Italy and abroad.

The **Museo storico dello studio** (the Historical Museum of the Studium), established for the University's eight hundredth anniversary in 1888, includes more than 250 documents, many mementoes (let us recall the Rector's insignia from the 16th century and Luigi Galvani's robe), and several portraits. The **Museo delle Navi** (Ships' Museum) and the **Collezione delle antiche carte geografiche** (Museum of Ancient Maps) are closely linked to the estab-

4

5

129

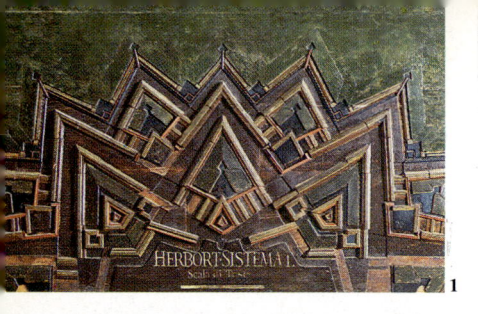

lishment of the *Geographical and Nautical Room* (1724): the first one presents ten very rare models of warships from the 17th and 18th centuries, such as *Le Royal Louis, Le Bien Aimé* (1771) and *Le Vainqueur*; the second museum exhibits important maps, engraved on copper, from the 17th century published in Bologna, Paris, Marseille, Amsterdam and in England.

Next to the Ships' Museum we can find the **Camera di Architettura Militare** (Military Architecture Room, divided up into two rooms) linked to the military career of Marsigli and to his unquenching thirst for knowledge. The first room is dominated at its centre by a big model of the town of Breisach; there are also other models of strongholds, a *vernetta*, a *military bridge*, an *ammunition cart*, large water-coloured panels and various models of old guns and mortars.

The **Museo Ostetrico «Giovanni Antonio Galli»** (Obstetrics Museum) is housed in the next rooms. It was founded in 1757 for Pope Benedict XIV, who had bought the scientific equipment of the famous surgeon Galli (1708-1782). The Museum is the reconstruction of an experimental laboratory, very exceptional for those times, which attests of the very high levels reached by obstetrics in the 18th century. There are also anatomical tables, clay, wood and wax models, and surgical instruments.

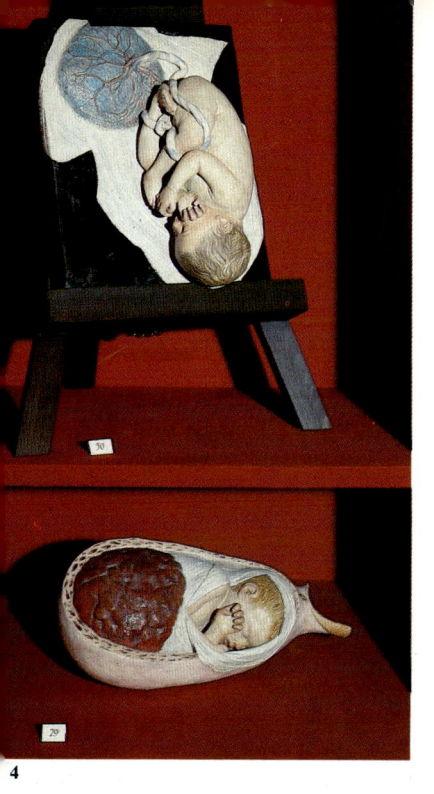

The **Museo di etnografia indiana e orientale** (Museum of Eastern and Indian Ethnography) has been recently rearranged. It was previously located in a section of the Archiginnasio razed during W. W II. It is formed by the items donated to the town by the scientist and patriot, Senator Francesco Pullé (1850-1934) which are very valuable for their artistical and historical importance. In the Rector's offices and in the University's Library, there is an important **paintings' Exhibition** with more than 600 valuable portraits, a collection started in 1754 with the 403 pieces bequeathed by Cardinal Filippo Maria Monti from Bologna. It includes portraits of cardinals, theologians, scientists, philologists, jurists, and men of letters; the authors are for the most part unknown. Let us mention the following: *Francesco Zanotti* by William Keeble; *Ludovico M. Montefani*, attributed to Angelo Crescimbeni; *Marco Antonio Collina Sbaraglia* by Donato Creti; *Self-portrait* by Lucia Casalini Torelli; *Giovanni Antonio Galli* by Crescimbeni; *Luigi Ferdinando Marsigli* by an unknown author, all of them in the Library. Also: *Benedict XIV* attributed to Carlo Vandi; *Eustachio Zanotti* attributed to Giampiero Zanotti; *Eustachio Manfredi*, a marble bust by Ercole Lelli; *Self-portrait* also by Ercole Lelli; *Laura Bassi* by Carlo Vandi; *Self-portrait* also by Vandi, all of them in the Rector's offices and in the Museums.

The **Museo di Astronomia** (Museum of Astronomy) is in the small tower and in the meridian room of the **Specola** (the entrance is at n. 31); it documents the progress in the observation of celestial bodies through a series of precious instruments used in the 18th and 19th centuries by the astronomers of the Institute of Sciences. Some of them had belonged to Marsigli. In the meridian room, set up in 1726, the following items are of remarkable interest: the brass and marble *meridian line* by Er-

1.2. Military architecture chamber: plastic models of fortified cities (detail). 3.4. A hall of the Obstetric Museum, and two models by Giovanni Antonio Galli. 5. The Meridian Room of the Specola (detail).

131

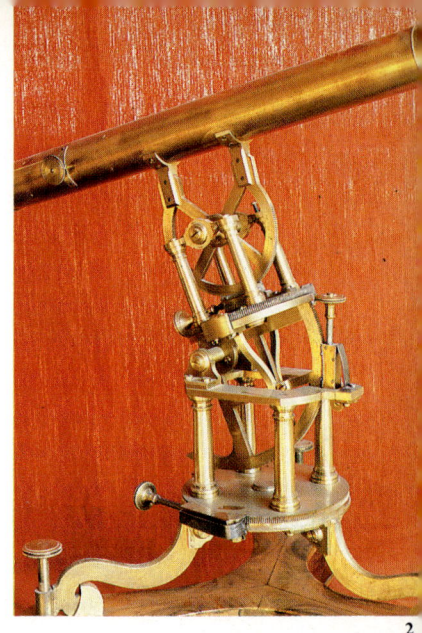

cole Lelli (1741), the *mobile quadrant* by Lusverg (1703), the *mobile quadrant* by Menini (1710), a *string meridian* from 1726, a *clock* by Quare (17th century), a *wall quadrant* by Sisson (1739). In the small tower, the evolution of the astronomic observation is attested by various instruments, such as the brass 16th-century *surveyor's cross*, a *plane astrolabe* (1565) by Gualtiero of Louvain, a *theodolite* by Paul Carré (17th century), a *sun-dial* by Bion from France (18th century), the eight metre *telescope* by Campani (17th century), and the *passages' instrument* (1739) by Jonathan Sisson from London. In the 18th century the imposing *Assembly Hall* of the Institute of Sciences was built right next to the northern flank of Palazzo Poggi. Planned by Dotti, it was inaugurated in 1756 after two decades of works. It is a section of the **Biblioteca Universitaria** (University's library) with entrance at n. 35, which comprises now more than 900,000 volumes and invaluable series of codices, manuscripts, incunabula, prints and drawings. The library includes also two precious scientific museums. The first one is the **Museo Aldrovandi**, set up here in 1907, which exhibits in 18th-century show-cases rare study materials collected by the famous naturalist Ulisse Aldrovandi from Bologna (1522-1605) and represents the remains of that first «museum» (16th century) already open to the public in the 18th century in Palazzo Pubblico. The water-coloured panels are gorgeous, and the cut wood blocks for printing are also quite interesting. Among the scientific items, let us recall the famous *Ranina Aldrovandi* (Aldrovandi's frog). The **Museo Marsigli**, set up in 1930, is connected with the Aldrovandi's one: it exhibits documents of the scientific activity of the great scientist from Bologna.

The University's museums in Palazzo Poggi are open every day (Monday excluded) from 9.30 a.m. to 12.30 p.m. and from 3.30 to 6.30 p.m. Guided tours on booking (tel. n. 512151).

1.2. Astronomy museum: ancient instruments (armillary sphere and telescope). 3. Carlo Francesco Dotti: Aula Magna of the Science Institute. 4. Marsigli Museum, with the monument to the scholar.

Museo di geologia e paleontologia «Giovanni Capellini» (Museum of Geology and Paleontology), in via Zamboni 63, is located in the rooms of the old Azzolini Hospital. Inaugurated in 1881, it is dedicated to the famous geologist and paleontologist from La Spezia (1833-1922), who was also rector of the university. It exhibits many important items from the collections of Aldrovandi (who founded the first museum of natural history in 1556), of Ferdinando Cospi (17th century) and Marsigli. Some show-cases date back to the 18th century. Among the items, all of exceptional quality, we would like to mention the following: fossils and rocks from the *Museum Metallicum* of Aldrovandi, already open to the public in 1648, an *Ichthyosaurus quadriscissus* from Germany; a *Mastodon alvernensis*; an *Ursus spelaeus* from Venezia Giulia; a *Glyptodon Typus* from Argentina; a *celidoterium capellinii* from South America; a giant model of *Diplodocus carnegiei*. Among the items from Bologna: remains of

Cetoteriophanes, a whale from the Pliocene, from S. Lorenzo in Collina, and the sirenid *Felsinotherium forestii*, from Riosto di Pianoro. The Museum hosts 150,000 specimens of invertebrates, 200 of vertebrates, 6,000 fossil plants, 15,000 rocks.

Museo di mineralogia e petrografia «Luigi Bombicci» (Museum of Mineralogy and Petrography), piazza di Porta S.Donato, 1. Located in a 1903 building (Engineer Pasquale Penza), it was set up in 1862 by Luigi Bombicci Porta who arranged also the collections. It is basically divided up into three sections: general mineralogy, with over 5,000 items and collections of meteorites and semi-precious stones;

1. Aldrovandi Museum, in the Hall of Benedict XIV. 2. A precious fossil: the «Aldrovandi Frog». 3. Zoology Museum: chamois ibex from Gran Paradiso diorama. 4. The brown bear, in the Parco d'Abruzzo diorama. 5. Atrium, with the Rhinoceros Unicornis and the Moon fish.

Regional Collections with over 12,000 specimens; sedimentary, magmatic and metamorphic rocks, and specimens of interest in the field of mining and studies of deposits. The collections of amber and precious stones are also of high quality. *For visits, please call n. 243556.*

Museo di zoologia (Museum of Zoology), via Francesco Selmi, 1; tel. n. 354188. It also comes originally from the collections of Aldrovandi (1556) with the addition of other collections made by Giuseppe and Gaetano Monti, by Camillo Ranzani and others. It still has the original layout arranged by Alessandro Ghigi who placed in this building from 1933 the old collections, the ones from the 19th century and the contemporary ones. The following items are of particular importance: the *fish collection* made by Ranzani, the *coral collection* of Marsigli, the *taxidermist preparations* from the laboratory (the *moonfish* and the *one-horn rhinoceros* are quite remarkable specimens), the *humming birds' collection* of Pius IX, the *shell collection* of Attilio Giovanardi, etc. The diorama and the teaching aids' collections have a high scientific interest. The big «sfargide» or *lute tortoise* is a gift from Benedict XIV.

Museo di antropologia (Museum of Anthropology), via Francesco Selmi, 1. Founded in 1908 by the famous anthropologist Fabio Frassetto, it exhibits a vast number of osteology materials of scientific interest to be used for educational purposes, by giving examples of the fundamental stages of the evolution process and the prehistoric cultures from the lower Paleolithic to the Neolithic: masks, models of busts, models of fossil primates, collections of skeletons of non-extint primates. There are also many specimens from the Region and the area of Bologna in particular.

Museo di anatomia comparata «Ercole Giacomini» (Museum of Comparative Anatomy), via Belmeloro 8. Set up in 1807 with the preparations of the famous physicians Germano Azzoguidi, Antonio Alessandrini and Gaetano Gandolfi, it exhibits preparations for injection (in coloured wax) of

back to the 18th and 19th centuries. The **Museo di patologia generale e anatomia patologica veterinaria** (Museum of Veterinary General Pathology and Pathologic Anatomy), via Belmeloro 10 (with beautiful full-size plastic models in wax, clay and plaster) and **Raccolte dell'istituto di patologia speciale e clinica chirurgica veterinaria** (Collections of the Institute of Special Pathology and Veterinary Surgery's teaching hospital), viale Quirico Filopanti 9, are naturally linked to the above-mentioned museum.

Museo di anatomia umana normale (Museum of Normal Human Anatomy), via Irnerio 48. It was firstly formed by the *collection of anatomical waxworks*, teaching aids that knew a phenomenal blooming in Bologna in the 18th century, linked to the fact that

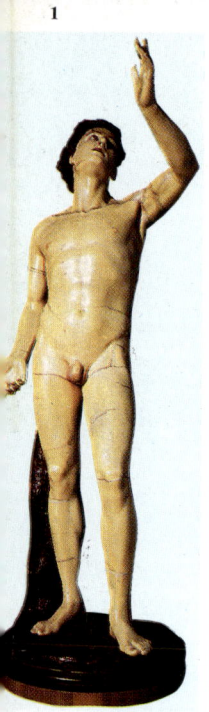

the arterial and venous system of mammals, and it has also a large exhibit of vertebrates' skeletons such as the one of the *Physeter macrocefalus*, a 20 metre-long sperm whale. The museum is named after the teacher who arranged the collections from 1903 to 1934.

Museo di anatomia degli animali domestici (Museum of Domestic Animals), via Belmeloro 12, established on the older *Museum of Veterinary* of Giacomo Gandolfi (1784), it was arranged by Clemente Papi in 1882 and later on improved and developed. It includes about two thousand anatomical preparations relative to all the tracts of domestic animals; many of these date

1. Wax museum: busts of the Manzolinis by Anna Morandi Manzolini. 2. Ercole Lelli: Adam and Eve. 3. Ercole Lelli: superficial and deep muscles. 4. Botanical Institute erected by Collamarini (1916).

it was then almost impossible for anatomy students to study on real bodies. The museum is usually called the *wax museum* because it exhibits the famous creations of wax artists who worked on live models. It was first set up as the *anatomy theatre of the Institute of Sciences* (1742) by Pope Benedict XIV. The Pope commissioned various anatomical pieces to the sculptor and anatomist Ercole Lelli (1702-1766), after having seen his two famous panels (shown here) of a *Normal kidney* and a *Horseshoe kidney*. The following works are magnificent under an artistic point of view: the group of eight full-size *statues of skinned people*, which illustrate the bundles of muscles running under the skin of men and women, displayed in beautiful 18th-century show-cases (it seems that for *Adam* and *Eve* Lelli was aided by Domenico Piò and Ottavio Toselli while Giovanni Manzolini participated in the creation of the other waxworks); by Anna Morandi Manzolini: *Self-portrait* (a bust) and the *Bust of her Husband, Giovanni Manzolini*, besides the really famous, and rightly so, *Hands*; by Giovanni Manzolini: the *Foetus with funicle and placenta*. The 19th-century waxworks by Clemente Susini and Giuseppe Astorri are also quite excellent. The museum was placed in here in 1907. The *Calori Collection* is also located in this building: thousand skulls from different periods and locations, which had been arranged and studied by the famous anatomist Luigi Calori (1807-1896): one of them is thought to be the skull of Athalarich, son of Amalasunta (the skeleton wore a medal of the Gothic king) and was therefore «authenticated» by Cardinal Oppizzoni after it was found in 1838 in Barbianello on the hills around Bologna.

Museo di fisica (Museum of Physics), via Irnerio 46, tel. 351099. It illustrates the history of physical sciences from the 18th century up to now, by stressing the link between the more recent equipment and the old devices in relation to mechanics, optics and acoustics. The following instruments are quite interesting: the *optical labora-*

tory of Giuseppe Campani (17th century), the *dark room* of Adams (18th century), the *planetarium* of Adams-Ferguson, a *model of a locomotive* from 1857, the 18th-century *teaching and experimental instruments* from the laboratories of Lord George Cowper, Augusto Righi and Quirino Majorana.

Orto botanico and erbario (Botanical Garden and Herbarium), via Irnerio 42, tel. 351301. Established in 1568 by Ulisse Aldrovandi, thus realizing a project by Luca Ghini, this garden was placed inside the Palazzo Pubblico and Terribilia made for it a tank that can be seen today in the Pinacoteca (Picture Gallery - see pag. ?). In 1803 it was moved to its present location near the Bentivoglio's Palazzina della Viola in accordance to a plan for a new University *campus* elaborated by Giovanni Battista Martinetti. In older times it was called *Garden of the simple* because only medicinal plants, called *simple medicines* (that is produced directly from plants), were grown there. Its present layout was arranged by Niccolò Giosuè Scannagatta and was further improved by the famous botanist Antonio Bertolari in the 19th century. It includes more than 2,000 species, of which many are grown under environmental conditions reproducing their places of origin. They are all extremely interesting: the Gymnosperm plants, medicinal plants from Italy, the wooded park, plants of the Mediterranean Region, the ornamental garden, fresh water environment, the Appennines' mesic woods, tropical plants and the magnificent green-house with the collection of cacti and succulents. The *Herbarium* includes several thousand specimens of dried plants: it is a collection known throughout Europe and it hosts also specimens dried by Aldrovandi in the 16th century, the large 18th-century collection of Giuseppe Monti, and the *hortus siccus florae italicae* - dried garden herbs of Italy - (with 30,000 specimens), arranged and filed by Bertoloni; also by Bertoloni is the *hortus siccus exoticus* - dried exotic garden herbs - and the *hortus siccus florae bononiensis* - dried garden herbs from Bologna.

Museo di anatomia e istologia patologica (Museum of Pathologic Histology and Anatomy), via Massarenti 9, tel. 391540: *it can be visited on Mondays and Wednesdays from 9 a.m. to 12.30 p.m. and on Saturdays from 10 a.m. to 1 p.m. (please call first).* Started up on the 18th and 19th centuries, it was placed here in 1948, and later restructured and rearranged by Prof. Paolo Scarani in 1983. It comprises mostly specimens and research studies on teratology (that is malformations) by the famous anatomist and pathologist Cesare Taruffi (Bologna 1821-1902); it exhibits many preparations in formalin or in sicco, and nice anatomical waxworks by Giuseppe Astorri and Cesare Bettini.

1. Botanical Gardens: exotic essences in the greenhouse. 2. Palazzo Davia Bargellini (16th C).

Civic Museum of Industrial Art, and Davia Bargellini Gallery

The grand home of Camillo Bargellini, without an arcade, as was often the custom for senatorial palaces, stands in strada Maggiore 44: the clear and pure façade, counterpointed by the cornices and the windows' jutting tympana, is characterized by a large portal - the only one of this genre in Bologna - flanked at each side by two telamones, which have contributed to the popular name of «palace of the giants» given to this building. Planned by Bartolomeo Provaglia in 1638 and built in about twenty years by the master builder Antonio Uri, Palazzo Davia Bargellini came into the hands of Virgilio Davia in 1839 and in 1876 to the Davia Bargellini Charitable Institution, established by Giuseppe Davia. The plastically modelled telamones, or atlantes, in «masegna» stone from the Appennines ranges near Bologna, were sculpted by Gabriello Brunelli (the right one) and Francesco Agnesini (the left one) and put in place in 1658. The open grand staircase from 1730, decorated with stucco works by Giuseppe Borelli, is the result of the elaboration of different projects made by Torreggiani, Dotti, and Conti. The **Civico Museo d'arte industriale** and the **Galleria Davia Bargellini** (the Civic Museum of Industrial Art and the Davia Bargellini Gallery) have been housed on the ground floor of the palace since 1924. In their layout, the seven rooms of the exhibition still reflect to a large extent the concepts on what a museum should be and offer which have inspired the museum's first curator, Francesco Malaguzzi Valeri, then supervisor of art galleries. The items of the Museum of Industrial Art are exhibited without any attempt to display them systematically preferring a more evocative outlook; the paintings, which demonstrate in their high-quality level the extent and variety of a single family's high art patronage, belong almost all to the Charitable Institution. Extensive restoration works were carried out in the Museum under the auspices of the Municipality in the years 1983-1984. The items on exhibit are more than one thousand. Room 1, furniture and rustic objects from Bologna from the 16th-17th centuries; of particular interest are the *scales* of the local Mint (from 1685 and 1786) and the collection of *albarelli* and other vases originally belonging to the «della Vita e della Morte» (of Life and Death) apothecary shops. Room 2, Renaissance furniture: a *bust of Gaspare Bargellini*, a terracotta work by Vincenzo Onofri; a *Virgin with Child*, also called *The Virgin of the Teeth*, a beautiful panel by Vitale da Bologna from 1345; the *Pietà*, a tempera work on a panel by Simone dei Crocefissi, 1368; *Virgin with Child*, a 15th-century panel, an early masterpiece by Bartolomeo Vivarini; four *wooden automata* from 1451, previ-

ously in the clocks' exhibition in the Municipal Palace; the *Mystical marriage of St. Catherine* by Innocenzo da Imola. The carved walnut *wedding chest* from the 16th-century school of Formigine is exquisite. Room 3: devotional object from the 17th and 18th centuries: in the room, set up as a noble family's chapel, there are sacred vessels and vestments, paintings and sculptures. Let us mention a *Crucifix* by Alessandro Algardi; the fine *Virgin with Child*, a polychromatic terracotta work by the school of Giuseppe Mazza. Room 4, middle-class 17th- and 18th-century furniture, furnishings, an important collection of terracotta sculptures: *Two Peasants*, and *Two Shepherds* by Angelo Piò; *Madonna*, *Fortitude*, *Apollo*, *Two Female Figures*, *Magdalene's Communion*: these are some of the works by Giuseppe Mazza to be found in this exhibition; among the many paintings, let us recall the *Crucifixion* by Calvaert and *Sisara's Death* by Franceschini. Room 5, magnificent Baroque furniture from the 17th and 18th centuries, as the *architectural chest of drawers* topped by a cabinet from the 16th centuries; the famous canvas with the three *Dice Players* by Giuseppe M. Crespi; the *Deposition* by Giuseppe M. Crespi; the *Carrier* and the *Hunter* by Luigi Crespi; a *Landscape* by Paul Brill; *Head of an Old Man* by Simone Cantarini; two *Portraits of a Man* by Domenico M. Canuti; *St. Francis of Assisi* by Mastelletta. Room 6, carved and gilded 17th- and 18th-century furniture: tables, easy-chairs, candelabra, ceremonial folding chairs, frames; an exquisite *ceremonial sedan-chair* in black painted wood from the 18th century; an interesting *18th-century a villa*, a reproduction in a very small scale

and really detailed. The following works hang on the walls: several paintings by Franceschini, Mirandolese and Bigari; *St. John the Baptist* by Mastelletta, *Crucifix with the Virgin and Saints* by Guido Reni, *Portrait of a Lady* by Luigi Crespi, *Portrait of a Bargellini Child* by Felice Torelli. Room 7, window display objects, ceramics, terracotta items: ceramics of Bologna and Emilia from the times of the Bentivoglio family to the end of the 16th century, Wedgwood, Saxonia, Capodimonte and Old Ginori porcelain, Murano glass; figurines of the nativity scene by Piò, Mazza and De Maria; embroideries from the 18th century; a fascinating *puppet theatre* originally belonging to the Albicini from Forlì and decorated with tempera painted scenes inspired by the Bibiena family, and 32 gorgeously dressed puppets, testifying to the theatrical taste common even in the family life of the Baroque *élites*.

The exhibit at Palazzo Davia Bargellini can be visited from 9 a.m. to 2 p.m. from Tuesday to Saturday; on Sunday from 9 a.m. to 12.30 p.m.; the museum is closed on Mondays and during holidays falling within the week.

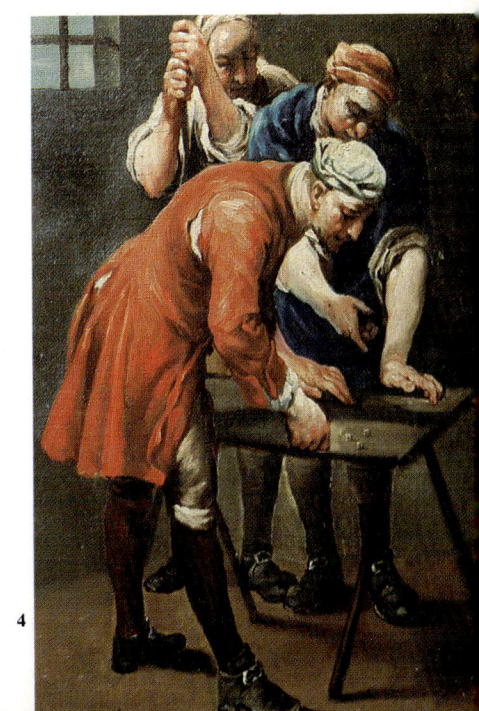

1. Davia Bargellini Museum: the festival carriage of the 18th century. 2. Two farmers made for a manger scene, of terracotta by A. Piò (18th C). 3. Puppet theater (18th C). 4. Giuseppe M. Crespi: dice players.

Didactic History Tapestry Museum

1. Via Barbiera: Palazzo Salina Brazzetti (18th C). 2. Historical Tapestry Museum: braiding loom (14th C). 3.4. Precious cloths. 5. Villa Spada: new residence of the Historical Tapestry Museum.

In via Barberia 13, the **Palazzo Salina Brazzetti** is a majestic and spectacular abode built by Carlo Francesco Dotti in 1720 for the Marquess Antonio Maria Monti Bedini. The façade was built also by Dotti in the years 1736-38. The inside was embellished with decorations by Ferdinando Bibiena and frescoes by Marcantonio Franceschini, Felice Cignani, Mariano Collina and others. The sculptures are by Giovanni Antonio Raimondi. The Historical and Didactic Museum of Tapestry and Upholstery has its seat here. This museum, which is a unique example of this kind in Italy, ranges among the most important in Europe. Founded and promoted by the master upholsterer Vittorio Zironi, it was opened in 1966; it is to be moved soon in the restored Villa Spada (see pag. 192). The collection, which comprises more than 6,000 pieces, exhibits only 4,000 of them in 12 rooms. It traces back the ancient tradition of hand-made and embroidered fabric by also illustrating the tools and equipment used in the workshops at the height of this activity. The items shown here are brocades, damask fabric, flag cloth, velvet, Jacquard and Gobelin weaving patterns, block-printed Indian cloth and hundreds of many other types of precious and artistic textiles; also old hand-looms, tools for upholstery and related objects (such as studs and tacks, trimmings, frames, blocks, borders, fringes, fittings, bands, etc.): an extraordinary display of materials ranging from the Early-Middle Ages to the Liberty style. Among the most valuable items, let us mention the following: 18th cent. silk wedding *sonnets*; a *brocatelle* cloth which covered the Christian images in the St. Sophia's Mosque in Istanbul; a *Lombard loom for trimmings* from 1380; a *lampasso* from the 8th century originally on the «golden altar» of S. Ambrogio church in Milan; a large *Lombard loom for textiles* from the 17th century; the moiré *canopy of the Madonna di S. Luca* from 1870; 50 *banners of the Arts' Guilds*, donated by the Municipality.

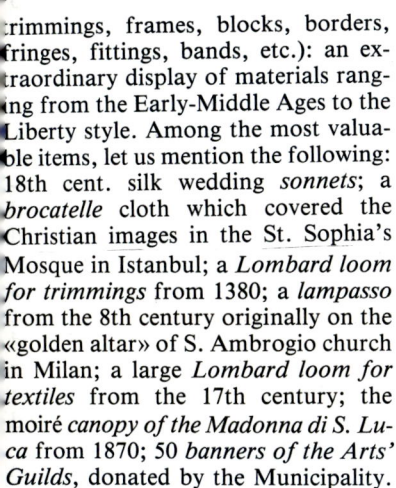

For visits to the museum, please call first tel. n. 331154 or 332346.

143

List of contents

Foreword	Page	3
History	»	6
1st Itinerary - *Summary*	»	10
2nd Itinerary - *Summary*	»	43
3rd Itinerary - *Summary*	»	64
4th Itinerary - *Summary*	»	87
The surroundings - *Summary*	»	98
Bologna's Museums - *Legend*	»	111